A Blandford
PET HANDBOOK

Cage Birds

A Blandford
PET HANDBOOK

Cage Birds

Joan Palmer

Blandford Press
POOLE · DORSET

First published in the U.K. 1983 by Blandford Press,
Link House, West Street, Poole, Dorset, BH15 1LL

Copyright © 1983 Blandford Books Ltd

Distributed in the United States by
Sterling Publishing Co., Inc.,
2 Park Avenue, New York, N.Y. 10016

British Library Cataloguing in Publication Data

Palmer, Joan
  Cage birds.—(A Blandford pet handbook)
  1. Cage birds
  I. Title
  636.6'86   SF461
         ISBN 0 7137 1203 1

Typeset by Megaron Typesetting, Boscombe, Bournemouth
Printed in Great Britain by Butler & Tanner Ltd., Frome and London

Contents

Acknowledgements

The author would like to express her thanks to the Pedigree Education Centre and to Spillers Foods Ltd (Caperns Advisory Service), in particular Mr Jon Delap, for invaluable assistance in the preparation of this book.

Grateful acknowledgement is also made to Miss Anita Lawrence, who provided the line drawings, and to the following who kindly loaned photographs: C. B. Studios (cover, figures 18, 19 and 25); Dr Alan Beaumont (figure 33); Graham Clarke (figure 9); R. Grantham (figure 27); Harry Lacey (figure 26); Press-tige Pictures (figures 1, 2, 10, 12, 13, 15, 16, 17, 28, 29 and 34).

Introduction

Why do you want a cage bird?

Many people in search of an affectionate, rewarding pet, look no further than a bird. Indeed, the practice of aviculture (rearing birds for pleasure) seems never to have been so popular for, as space becomes limited and the number of people living in flats increases, so does the demand for a pet which does not need a garden, will not preclude its owner from going out to work and makes far less demands on their time than a dog or cat. Also, of course, a pet bird is far less likely to fall foul of a landlord should you live in rented accommodation as, being confined to a cage, it is unlikely to cause any damage, or to inconvenience other tenants in any way. Cleaning the cage is a simple task and takes only a little time. Moreover, there is not much waste to dispose of, which is another advantage for flat-dwellers.

Birds do not cost a great deal to keep and are usually happy and healthy throughout their long lives. Children love them and they have proved of great therapeutic value to the elderly and to folk living alone. Of course, because birds live in cages inside the home, it does not matter one jot if there is a busy road outside as they are not going to rush across it and get run over.

Undoubtedly a bird is a most suitable pet for people who go out to work but if all members of the household are out all and every day, it is best to buy a couple of birds which can then keep each other company. Pets, like people, are miserable if left alone for lengthy periods. Where a family member is predominantly home-based, however, the single bird will happily regard its human companion as a substitute bird.

Choosing your bird

Budgerigars

By far the most popular pet bird, and certainly the easiest to keep, is the Budgerigar. In the USA, it is known as the Parakeet, because it is, after all, a member of the Parrot family.

Budgerigars make delightful companions; they soon settle down as part of the family, are playful, intelligent and truly can be taught to speak. Indeed, with patience and perseverance, a baby Budgerigar can be taught its first words within 6 weeks and thereafter additional phrases can be added to its vocabulary.

Canaries

The Canary has been a popular pet bird for centuries and is renowned for its beautiful song. The Roller Canary, in particular, excels in its singing ability, but remember, if you want a canary that will sing, you must purchase a male. Although one tends to think of the Canary as a yellow bird, a number of colours and varieties have now been developed. Like Budgerigars, they breed easily and are healthy and easy to look after.

Zebra Finches

If an attractive little foreign bird appeals, you need look no further than a Zebra Finch. Ever since they were first imported into the UK, Zebra Finches have been high on the list of favourite aviary birds because of their attractive ways and the freedom with which they breed. Another point in their favour—they make excellent foster parents for some of the rarer foreign birds, especially straying Finches, due to their highly-developed parental instincts.

Parrots

Parrots have been domesticated for years but, in recent times, seem to have discarded their Long John Silver image for the more fashionable role of companion to show business people and the smart social set.

The most popular Parrots are African Greys, which are the best talkers and, if you are not careful, pick up rather naughty vocabulary.

Senegal Parrots also have the gift of mimicry, but their intonation cannot compete with that of their African counterparts.

Men and women living alone are advised to choose a Parrot of the opposite sex as male Parrots prefer the company of women and vice versa, a trait which is not as uncommon as you might think in the pet-owning world. Parrots are extremely long-lived and make ideal companions, but, if you want a Parrot to talk, it is essential to buy a tame one and advisable to choose one that has been bred in captivity as it will be far more amenable to training.

Mynah Birds
Another firm favourite is the Mynah Bird which is also a prodigious talker. Indeed, the Mynah Bird is so fond of its own voice and of human company that it can prove rather noisy, so it would be unfair to buy one if you are unlikely to appreciate the company it will wish to bestow on you.

There are one or two disadvantages to Mynah-owning, Mynahs are softbills and eat fruit and soft food; the resultant droppings are loose and messy, so you must be prepared, if you choose a Mynah, to do a certain amount of housekeeping in return for your entertainment . . . and entertain the Mynah will, to the extent of repeating embarrassing phrases oblivious to the presence of, say, the Vicar!

Expense and commitment

The prices which pets command tend to vary not only between town and country,but also according to popularity, supply and demand. Suffice it to say that, if you are thinking in terms of a Parrot or Mynah which is a prolific talker, you will incur an outlay similar to that of the buyer of a winning show dog, whereas if a Budgerigar or one of the other smaller birds has taken your fancy, the price would more realistically compare with that of a rabbit or other small caged pet. On top of the purchase price, you must budget for the cost of the cage and feeding. As far as Budgerigars, Canaries and Zebra Finches are concerned, the simple wood and wire cages are quite adequate and very reasonable in price. Metal cages are more expensive but are essential if you intend to keep a Parrot or Mynah Bird. As far as these birds are concerned, it is worth spending a little extra to ensure that the cage is secure and the metal is well-finished.

The cost of feeding and maintaining your bird should amount to not much more a week than the price of a bar of chocolate. Again, Parrots and Mynahs are the more expensive because they require fruit in their diet. If you have adequate storage facilities, seed and grit can be bought in bulk.

The most serious commitment you must be prepared to make is one of time: time to check your bird on several occasions each day; to attend to feeding and cleaning; to arrange,when necessary, for veterinary care; and to ensure that, if you do have to go away on business or take a holiday, your pet will be cared for in your absence. Finally,there must be a willingness to give the bird consideration and love, a commodity which such companions cannot ask for but which every pet richly deserves.

1
Budgerigars

Origins

The Budgerigar (*Melopsittacus undulatus*) is a native of Australia, where it lives and breeds in huge flocks among the eucalyptus groves of New South Wales, Victoria and Western Australia. Records show that the Budgerigar was first brought to England in 1840, after being introduced to almost every country of the world. There was, in the early days, a high mortality rate, due mainly to ignorance but, by 1855, Budgerigars were being successfully bred in Germany, and the USA and Japan soon followed suit.

In the wild, the Budgerigar makes its home in a tree and often more than one family resides in the root area of one eucalyptus. It enjoys the company of its own kind, which is why it breeds best if kept in an aviary. Its clannishness is an advantage in the face of danger, for a Budgerigar sighting a predator will immediately warn its fellows, whereupon the entire flock will take to the sky.

The captive Budgerigar tends to grow larger than its Australian cousin and selective breeding has resulted in a variety of colours.

Choosing and buying your bird

Obviously you want a Budgerigar which is not only attractive and healthy but likely to reward you with many years of friendship. You should therefore buy from a reliable source rather than acquire the first Budgerigar you see in a shop window. By all means choose from a good pet-shop if you wish, but be sure that it belongs to the relevant pet-trade association, that the pets on sale are all lively and healthy and that they are kept in clean quarters with adequate food and water.

Alternatively, you may prefer to get your budgerigar from a breeder advertising in the local paper, or via the columns of the fanciers' publications, *Cage and Aviary Birds* or *American Cage Bird Magazine*. In case of difficulty, a letter to the Budgerigar Society or a word with the secretary of your local Cage Bird Club (easily contact-

Figure 1   The Lutino Budgerigar did not appear as a strain in Britain until 1884

able through a reference library) should quickly put you on the right track.

There is a lot to be said for both pet-shop and private purchase. The pet-shop will wish to retain you as a regular customer, while the breeder/exhibitor has a reputation to uphold and will naturally like to think that the stock is destined for a good home and may also bring him/her credit in exhibition.

If, as most people do, you want a Budgerigar which you can teach

Figure 2 It is among the Violet Budgerigars, such as this specimen, that the most brilliantly coloured birds are to be found

to talk, choose a young cock or hen between 6 and 9 weeks old. Apart from a few special varieties, such as Albinos and Lutinos, whose ages can only accurately be gauged by an expert, young birds up to the age of 3 months have distinctive characteristics which aid identification. There are bars (striations) across the head with flecking, rather than clearly defined throat spots, on the bib of the mask (lower face). Young cocks have a bold purplish cere (the fleshy part at the base of the beak) and young hens have a bluish/white cere. There is no white ring (iris) around the eye at this age.

At about 3 months of age,the baby feathers are moulted at the onset of adult plumage. The cock bird's cere changes to a deep shiny blue and the hen's to a definite brown and both sexes develop a white iris around the eye. Once the adult plumage has been assumed, it is impossible to determine a Budgerigar's age accurately unless it carries a dated closed ring on one leg, fitted by the breeder.

Generally, aviary-bred birds are banded with the date of hatching and, indeed, in some areas, this is a legal requirement as proof that Budgerigars, and other members of the Parrot family, have been bred in captivity.

You may be offered an older bird and, while a few days over 9 weeks makes little or no difference, it does become progressively more difficult, as a Budgerigar gets older, to train it and to teach it to talk. A Budgerigar of 9 months or more, with no previous training, may never talk, although such a bird may well settle down to become a lovable and friendly companion. Birds which have been kept in an aviary up to this time—especially hens—are likely to prove even more difficult.

You should look for a quiet bird with a bright eye and all its feathers intact. Make sure the plumage lies tight to its body and that the vent is unsoiled. The colour of the Australian imports was light green, with yellow mask and black and yellow markings on the wings. However, there are now many colour varieties, the most exotic obviously proving most expensive and it is worth mentioning that some of these have not proved to be quite so hardy as the more commonly seen greens and blues.

Pet Budgerigars, if well looked after, usually live for about 7 or 8 years. However, with advances in veterinary science, and as more is learnt about their care, their lifespan does appear to be increasing and claims have been made of individual Budgerigars living for 20 years or more.

Accommodation

Your Budgerigar will be happiest in a roomy, well-sited cage that is not cluttered with toys. The best position for the cage is opposite a window, away from a door and no higher than about 120 cm (48 in) off the floor. It may be of wood or metal construction and ideally should be fitted with perches of hazel, or any fruit tree wood, varying in diameter from 10 mm (³⁄₈ in) to 18 mm (³⁄₄ in) to exercise the feet. Once the cage is sited it is better not to move it. Two Budgerigars can be kept in an ordinary bird cage as long as they are allowed out to fly around the room occasionally, but obviously you should obtain the largest cage possible.

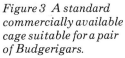

Figure 3 A standard commercially available cage suitable for a pair of Budgerigars.

Above: *Figure 4 A few toys will keep your Budgerigar amused but do not overcrowd the cage with playthings*

There are two basic types of cage, one constructed entirely of wire and the other of wood with a wire front. The latter has the advantage of being cheaper and easier to construct and affording its occupants some protection from draughts. There are also various circular cages on the market which, regrettably, are not always as practical as they are pleasing to the eye.

Hygiene

A Budgerigar prefers cool, well-ventilated surroundings, so do try and avoid draughts and direct sunlight. Clean the cage, feeding pots, perches and toys with a disinfectant or a very weak solution of bleach once a week, rinsing and drying off before re-assembly. Renew the sandsheet or loose sand covering the floor. One popular brand of sand sheet comes in a handy tear-off roll. This fits all standard-sized cages and greatly simplifies cage cleaning. The cage can be lightly covered during the evening or at night to ensure that your pet is undisturbed once it has roosted.

Feeding

Basic food for the Budgerigar is a mixture of canary seed and millet. One well known product in the UK is treated with iodine to guard against thyroid deficiency, a rather common complaint among Budgerigars kept as pets.

The seed pots, which were probably provided with the cage, should be regularly filled and the accumulated husks should be blown off each day. Never attempt to vary the food intake without expert advice. Seed, cuttlefish bone, budgerigar grit and fresh drinking water should always be available to your pet. *These items are vital.*

Most budgerigars do appreciate titbits occasionally, such as spray millet, carrot, spinach, lettuce, chickweed, seedling grasses and apple. Green food should be well washed, drained and fed sparingly on two or three mornings a week. Feed small quantities and remove the remains at the end of the same day.

Millet sprays are not essential for a Budgerigar in fit condition and can be withheld when a bird is not eating its loose millet—at other times a spray should be offered once a week as a treat. Branded millet sprays, in packs of at least three, are selected from the finest Chinese and Italian crops.

Foods prepared for human beings are quite unsuitable for Budgerigars and some could prove dangerous. When the bird is moulting or otherwise below par, cow's milk diluted 50/50 with water may be offered. Change this daily or more frequently in hot weather.

Different seed grasses form the diet of the wild Budgerigar which is why the foods mentioned, fundamentally cultivated grasses, are most readily accepted by the domesticated bird. However, some items, although they may be on offer in pet-shops, are not particularly kind to the Budgerigar's digestion, e.g. hard-hulled Dakota millet from America and golden millet, which is usually too hard for young Budgerigars. Japanese millet, when available, is suitable and so is mohair millet from India.

Cuttlefish bone is particularly beneficial because it provides calcium and phosphorus. Also the mere act of pecking at it will help to prevent the bird's beak overgrowing and it is a good idea to fix a piece of cuttlefish bone to the cage. Your Budgerigar will be far better occupied pecking at something of this nature than by having so many toys that it cannot fly around the cage.

Training

When you let your pet out of its cage, do not forget to close windows and doors, protect any open fire place, cover up any house plants, *draw net curtains across any clear glass to prevent accidents* AND put out the cat if you have one.

In the early days of unfamiliar freedom, a Budgerigar can be retrieved by first darkening the room, drawing the curtains if need be, and then seeking it out with a torch. Use a hat or something similar to capture the bird and then, with one hand, envelop its wings close to its body whilst engaging your thumb and forefinger on each side of the head under the cheek bones. Holding the bird thus, you can pop it back into its cage. Later, your pet will return voluntarily, sometimes when commanded to do so.

If your Budgerigars are kept in an aviary, try not to handle them too often. They are timid by nature and disturbance upsets them. If, however, you are keeping one as a household pet you will naturally want to form a close relationship with it. The first step is to gain its confidence. Do not bring your Budgerigar home and expect to make friends with it immediately. Allow it to settle down for a couple of days, then approach the cage very quietly repeating 'Pretty Boy' or some similar two-word phrase. Once your approach is accepted without fear you can commence finger training. Extend the index finger alongside a perch, raising it under the bird's breast until it hops on.

Figure 5 By gently nudging the breast, you will soon persuade your bird to step onto your finger

Move your hand slowly around the cage transferring your pet from perch to perch, whispering encouraging noises. In a day or two, you will be able to withdraw your hand from the cage with the bird perched on your finger. Try stroking down its beak with the index finger of your other hand. It is all good confidence-winning training. Continue repeating the two-word phrase as often as possible and very soon your patience will be rewarded. Your pet will have said its first few words. Add another phrase and repeat this until he can say it perfectly. In this way, you can build up an extensive vocabulary for your bird.

A baby Budgerigar can, with patience, be taught to repeat its first words in about 6 weeks. Any bird which is not taught to speak during the first 9 months of its life is unlikely to do so—but it is not impossible!

Breeding

To breed Budgerigars successfully requires not only ample knowledge of the needs of the birds but also careful attention to their welfare throughout the year. The breeder who does little more than supply his birds with seed and water, carrying out only perfunctory cleaning for most of the year, cannot hope to get his birds to peak condition by taking an interest in them only a week or two before breeding operations commence. Strict attention must be paid to their diet and cleanliness throughout the year.

Budgerigars will go to nest at any time of the year provided that they are in breeding condition. The breeder must be guided, therefore, not so much by the calendar but by whether or not his birds are ready. While breeding is sometimes begun very early in the year, it is usual practice in the UK to wait until about March. Do not, on any account, pair up birds that are not ready to breed, for the result will only be a refusal to nest, or else the hen will produce infertile eggs.

How can you tell when the birds are in breeding condition? Reliable signs in a cock will be a bright blue cere, a vigorous and lively attitude, tapping of the perch and wire netting, calling to the hen if the sexes are separated and continual attempts to feed her.

The cere of the hen is rich brown when she is in breeding condition, and she will respond to the calls of the cock. If separated by wire netting she will cling to it and await his attentions. She will usually gnaw all available woodwork and may also drop eggs from the perches.

The most important points to remember are *not* to breed with birds that are: a) out of condition, b) have been ailing, c) show any signs of moulting, d) are too young.

Special accommodation

In order to breed, Budgerigars need nest boxes and it will generally be found most convenient to hang or screw such a box onto the back of the breeding cage. Each breeding cage should be 90×30 cm (36×12 in) in area and 45 cm (18 in) high. If preferred, double- or treble-sized cages can be made and divided into single compartments with the aid of sliding plywood panels.

One nest box that has many advantages is the pull-out type which, in effect, is a box without a top sliding loosely into a box without a front. Other types of nest box with lids on top or flaps at the front are also popular.

The advantages of a pull-out type box lie in its safety and simplicity. There is, for instance, less danger of a chick being injured when a lid is closed after inspection as, to open the box, it is only necessary to insert the forefinger into the entrance hole and completely withdraw the inner box from the outer. The box can be carried around the bird

room and put down at any convenient spot for cleaning purposes or
for ringing chicks, with no fear of the eggs or chicks falling out.

The interior of the nest box must be fitted with a concave bottom as
this is the nearest equivalent to the bored-out or natural holes in trees
which Budgerigars use in the wild. No other nesting material is
required, although a wooden step or block may be placed below the
entrance hole so that the hen does not land directly on the eggs. In
this case, the concave bottom should be off-set and well clear of the
entrance hole; this arrangement is not essential, however, and the
concave bottom can fill the whole base area of the box. It is normally
14 cm (5½ in) square.

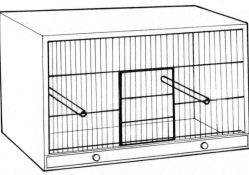

Right: *Figure 6 The
breeding cage
should be fitted with
a nest box*

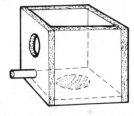
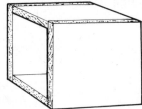

Left: *Figure 7 A
nest box of the pull-
out type, with a
concave block at the
bottom on which the
eggs can be
deposited safely, is
ideal*

The entrance hole should measure about 4.5 cm (1¾ in) and not less
than 3.8 cm (1½ in) in diameter. The all-round measurements of the
nest box (with 5 cm [2 in] stepping block) should be 19 cm (7½ in) long,
14 cm (5½ in) wide and 18−20 cm (7−8 in) high. Breeders sometimes
like to sprinkle a little sawdust on the bottom of the nest box, possibly
in the hope that the hen will not bite at the wooden concave bottom;
hens have a habit of doing this during the period when the eggs are
being laid and it is an instinctive reaction. She will soon stop once the
eggs are hatched. Most nest boxes are fitted with a short perch about
5 cm (2 in) below the entrance hole but this is not essential.

Pairing

The sex of a Budgerigar can be determined by the colour of the cere or wattle which lies above the beak and surrounds the nostrils. In blue and green cocks, this is of a bright blue colour while, in the hen, it varies from whitish to a deep rich brown, according to the condition of the bird. The colour of the cere becomes paler when the hen is out of condition. An ailing cock will quite often show a brownish tinge over the blue colouration.

Young hens often have a faint blue tinge at 6 weeks of age but the colours are fairly recognisable at 12 weeks. The blue colouration in a young cock continues down into the nostrils whereas, in the young hen, the interior and edges of the nostrils are much paler in colour than the rest of the wattle; it requires a keen eye and experience to be certain, however.

Lutinos, Albinos and Fallows, as previously indicated, are difficult to sex, even when adult. Although, at all ages, the cere is of varying shades of brown, it usually has a bluish tinge in the male birds. This may not be easy for the novice to recognise.

Budgerigars should not be mated until they are about 1 year old; 10 months for a cock and 11 months for a hen are recommended ages.

While some cocks remain potent and can fertilise eggs over a period of years, hens quite often become unreliable after their third season, letting their eggs become chilled or neglecting their chicks. This is not always the case, however, and some hens have proved to be exemplary mothers until 6 years of age. Two ageing Budgerigars should not be paired but should each be provided with young mates.

If you have several birds and you are breeding with exhibiting in mind, remember that the best cock should be paired with the best hen and so on down the scale of quality. Before putting the birds together, they should be compared side by side in show cages to find out whether they possess the same fault or faults and, if so, a more suitable partner should be found for each of them. Faults to be avoided are small heads, small throat spots, crossed or dropping wings and lack of size or falling away of the back of the skull. Some of these faults may be cancelled out by the other bird; for instance, a bird with crossed wings may be safely paired with another whose wings are inclined to drop. Both faults in all probability will be corrected in some of the young.

Never waste a really good cock on a mediocre hen or vice versa as this only leads to poor results in terms of quality.

Nesting and incubation

The nest boxes should be put up a few days after pairing, or when it is
obvious that the birds are on amicable terms. The first egg will be laid
about 10 days later and the hen will then lay on alternate days until
the clutch is complete. The incubation period is usually 18 days
beginning from the day the first egg is laid. Sometimes, however, the
hen will wait for the second day before starting to sit, so it is advisable
to reckon on 20 days before the first egg hatches.

The average number of eggs in a clutch is four to five although any
number up to nine is possible. Nowadays, four eggs in the first clutch
and four or five in the second is considered quite satisfactory.

Because the hen Budgerigar lays on alternate days, it can be readily
seen that, in a clutch of five, the eldest chick will be 8 days old by the
time the youngest hatches out. This is perfectly natural, but not desirable for the breeder because usually the youngest and weakest nestlings die. A chick that dies must be removed promptly before it decomposes. Daily inspection for this and any other trouble is advisable.

Feeding

Chicks are fed by a process of regurgitation. The parent projects a
stream of pre-digested food into the crop of the baby bird, which is
why it is called 'crop milk'. While the hen is sitting, she does all the
feeding of the chicks and the cock feeds her. Once out of the nest
box, the chicks are fed by both parents.

While the chicks are being reared offer the parents chickweed, lettuce or seedling grasses in addition to their normal seed, making
sure that they are quite clean and fresh. They also like pecking
greenstuff.

Seed soaked in water for 48 hours and partially germinated is also
a valuable supplement. The surplus water should be drained away
before the seed is fed to the birds. Cod liver oil may be given daily.
Finally make sure that a supply of fresh water is always available.

Care of young birds

Hygiene: Once the chicks are being reared, you must keep an eye on
their beaks and claws in case they become caked with hardened
matter, resulting from the poor feeding and dirty habits of their
parents. Most birds by nature are conscientious about keeping their

nests clean, but one occasionally comes across a bird that pumps regurgitated food over the chicks' faces and into the nest; this, mixed with excreta and scattered seed, mixes into a cement-like substance which sticks to their claws and beaks. A daily inspection of the nest box will show up this state of affairs and the following action is suggested.

Moisten the chicks' toes or beaks with warm water before attempting to remove the hard lumps, taking care not to use force, otherwise claws may be torn out. (Claws removed this way do not grow again.) Similarly, careful attention must be given to the beak. Unless it is cleaned regularly, it is likely to become deformed.

As to the actual nest box, when dirty feeding is evident this will have to be cleaned out fairly frequently. An old teaspoon, with one edge sharpened, is an admirable tool for scraping the concave bottom, which may be covered with a fresh layer of sawdust after cleaning. The chicks can be handled without any ill effect and, during cleaning operations, can be placed in another box reserved for this purpose, as long as they are returned to their own box afterwards without delay.

Fledging: All being well, young Budgerigars emerge from the nest box at between 4 and 5 weeks of age, fully feathered and able to fly, but the breeder should not be in too great a hurry to remove them from their parents. Whilst some precocious youngsters can 'crack' seed after only a day or so out of the box, some cannot cope for several days and the cock continues to feed them until they are self sufficient. As a guide, it is advisable not to remove the young from their parents until they have been out of the nest for a week or 10 days.

A few days before the first youngsters leave the box,the hen will commence to lay her second clutch. There is no need for concern about this as the hen will see to the safety of the eggs. Incubation, hatching and rearing will proceed normally as for the first clutch and will continue to do so as long as the nest box remains in position. It is the general opinion among experienced breeders that two clutches should be the limit for any one season, especially if the total number of chicks reared amounts to eight or nine. However,if only very few chicks have been reared from the first two clutches, it is generally thought that a third clutch will not be harmful.

Assuming that a total of eight chicks have been reared in two clutches, when the last of the second clutch has left the nest, the box should be removed. If any more eggs have been laid they should be given to other parents who have not been so prolific.

Do not remove the hen from the breeding quarters immediately, however, but allow her to remain with the cock and her family until the chicks are removed. The parents can then be returned to their normal quarters.

Ringing: If a pedigree record is being kept, the young birds should be ringed when they are 5 or 6 days old. This is essential for identification, particularly if some chicks, for any reason, are given to foster parents (unless, of course, the clash, such as a yellow chick among a collection of blues, makes it obvious). As a rule, Budgerigars make good foster parents and, if chicks should vary considerably in size in any one brood, transfers to other nest boxes to even out the sizes may be desirable.

The ring authorised by the Budgerigar Society in the UK is the closed metal ring. The American Budgerigar Society has traceable bands. Breeders generally become expert at the somewhat tricky operation of slipping the band over the front toes of the Budgerigar, but it is a finicky procedure and the owner of an unbanded bird, who wishes it to be ringed for identification, would be well advised to ask a veterinary surgeon to do it.

Figure 8 Fitting a closed metal ring on a bird's foot is a tricky business

Aviary breeding

If the birds are to breed in an aviary, it is a good plan to keep each pair in a separate cage for a week or more before introducing them to the breeding quarters, in the hope that they will become so attached to one another that they will form a true love match, remaining faithful throughout the breeding season. Regrettably, it is not unusual for cock Budgerigars to stray, especially when their chosen mate is incubating the eggs.

Indeed, when a large number of birds are kept in an aviary, indiscriminate mating is usually inevitable and the chance of keeping accurate pedigree records is almost non-existent. The system of keeping several pairs together is known as 'the colony system' and has the added disadvantage that the hens are liable to squabble or fight over the nest boxes. Breeding time brings out the worst of the hen Budgerigar's character and sometimes the fighting is so spiteful that it can lead to the wholesale destruction of eggs, or even chicks, should a hen stray into a neighbour's nest box. Therefore, if colony breeding is practised, make sure that there are more boxes than breeding pairs and place them all at the same height, if possible inside the sleeping quarters and high up on the wall. Should two hens quarrel over the same box, remove it altogether and they will soon select one each for themselves.

For the reasons given, it is clear that the fancier wishing to exercise complete control over his birds' pedigree, must keep each pair in a separate cage or separate compartment of the aviary.

Exhibiting your bird

The Fancy

Often after joining a fanciers' club and making friendships with other owners, newcomers, particularly if they have started an outdoor aviary collection, may, after their first year of breeding, decide to test the quality of their stock by showing.

Many such people do not show their birds because they have no idea how to go about it and usually Budgerigars sold and kept as pets are no match for a skilled breeder's birds. Therefore, the pet-owner would be wise to seek a show which schedules a class or classes for 'pet' Budgerigars. At smaller shows, a special class may not be scheduled—although there is often one for 'Any Variety of Pet Bird'. This may seem unfair, but usually the exhibits are appraised on fitness and cage presentation.

To get a better understanding of exhibiting, it is essential first to learn something about the structure of the Budgerigar Fancy. At the head of the Fancy in the UK is the Budgerigar Society, generally called the 'parent body'. It has eleven area societies affiliated to it, each one responsible for members in its own area. One of the advantages of membership is the registration of a code number and the issue of closed coded rings to identify breeders. The Society assists all who are interested in Budgerigars and also acts as a parent body in a closely-knit international organisation.

There are also local Budgerigar societies and mixed variety cage bird societies as well as various national specialist societies catering for a particular kind or group of Budgerigars.

In the USA, the parent body is the American Budgerigar Society. It has seventeen regional groups and is affiliated with fifty-seven Societies, taking in breeders, owners, exhibitors and experimenters while, in common with the British society, it sponsors and provides patronage for competitive exhibitions and maintains standards of perfection for the species.

Figure 9 This Budgerigar, in an exhibition cage, shows the 'normal' feather characteristics as found in wild Budgerigars in their native Australia

Shows

Open shows: You do not need to be a member of the promoting society to exhibit at these shows. In the UK, every November, the Budgerigar Society stages the biggest show of Budgerigars in the world, attracting in excess of 4000 entries. The standard is usually very high.

Cage and Aviary Birds, the fanciers' weekly newspaper, promotes the National Exhibition of Cage and Aviary Birds annually in December. This is a show of world renown for Canaries, British birds, Budgerigars and foreign birds, as well as talking birds.

The area societies more often stage an annual open show—and sometimes a show earlier in the year for members' young birds. Many local societies—there are about 1000 of them in the UK—stage an open show. This greatly increases the number of events in the show calendar, which extends from about July to mid-January. It is usual for the national specialist Budgerigar societies to hold their annual event in conjunction with a major open show.

Member shows: Such shows are restricted to fully paid up members and are much smaller affairs, often held in church halls, schools, community centre halls or even a room above a pub on a Saturday or Sunday afternoon. Most local societies stage three events a year, roughly April/May, August/September and November/December.

These are called: Nest-Feather shows—for young birds not yet moulted into adult plumage; Young Stock shows—for fully moulted birds of current-year breeding; the Annual shows—for birds of any age.

Patronage: All promoting societies offer special awards which can be competed for in higher competition by a bird gaining a first prize in its class. (This does not apply to pet birds.) Sometimes the award will be a rosette, a cup or trophy, some other insignia and/or a small cash prize.

Patronage is interchanged throughout the Fancy by the offering of these special awards by one or more societies to the promoting society's show. A small fee is charged to enter a bird into a show and modest prize money, usually on a sliding scale, can be won by the fortunate few who are successful

At many of the shows patronised by the Budgerigar Society, a further cash award can be won by birds wearing an official closed-coded ring on one leg, denoting the year of issue, the breeder's code number and a series number. Such rings can only be bought by members of the Budgerigar Society or an area society and are issued for the current year on 1st January and thereafter each year.

Entering a show

First find your show. It is usual for an open show to be advertised some weeks in advance in *Cage and Aviary Birds* or *American Cage Bird Magazine* and/or the respective bulletins of the Budgerigar Society or the American Budgerigar Society, giving the venue, the show secretary's name and address, and other relevant information. A telephone call or a postcard to the Secretary will elicit the schedule and entry form in the post as well as the show rules, classes, judges, prize money, patronage, special awards and much else to enable an intending exhibitor to properly complete the entry form. This should be returned by the specified date and the entry delivered to the show hall on time.

From time to time, a full list of the year's events is published in the editorial columns of the Fancy's papers intended for those exhibitors who like to plan well in advance.

Member shows are rarely advertised. Anyone wanting to show at these local events must first join the promoting society. Here again, *Cage and Aviary Birds* and *American Cage Birds Magazine* carry a fairly comprehensive list of society activities, usually under the heading of 'Club News', giving the venue, the date of the meeting and the subject matter. By joining a local society and attending a couple of meetings, a great deal of information will be forthcoming concerning the shows and other matters of interest.

Preparing your bird for a show

Breeders take a great deal of trouble to exhibit their birds in prime condition. It is said to be an art in itself. The exhibit, to do itself justice, must be steady in the cage, clean, fit and with its full complement of feathers intact and lying smooth to the body. Budgerigars, however, frequently moult a few feathers during most of the year (they also have a light head moult in the spring and a full moult in October) and it is sometimes difficult to find all the intended exhibits ready at one time. This applies equally to the single pet-bird owner who must judge a couple of weeks in advance whether the Budgerigar will be in prime exhibition condition.

The six throat spots carried by most varieties of the Budgerigar are

Opposite: *Figure 10   A Pied Budgerigar*

its 'shop window' and as such assume great importance to judges and breeders alike. Whereas the loss of one feather elsewhere may pass unnoticed, an absent spot feather sticks out like a sore thumb. Such a bird, if it is sent to a show, will be suitably penalised, so the challenge is to possess a bird, or birds, of some exhibition merit, select a suitable show, and prepare them to look their best in order to find favour with the judge.

Pet-bird exhibitors need not worry unduly about special preparation. The normal wire cage sould be cleaned and not cluttered with too many toys or decorations. However, the bird should be fit. The cock bird's cere should be a deep shiny blue while that of a hen should be a crusty dark brown.

The feathers can be cleaned and encouraged to lie smoothly by daily spraying with warm water in a plastic handspray. If possible, it is best to find a show which coincides with the Budgerigar's natural high condition, rather than try to promote this condition artificially. Cover the cage in transit to avoid fright and draughts.

Breeders should take more pains to prepare their birds for a particular show. Some 8 weeks in advance of the show, the intended exhibits should be brought in from the aviary and put into a stock cage—usually a double breeding cage with the slide partition removed. Each bird should be examined for damaged or broken flight and tail feathers and these should be carefully removed so that they will regrow in time for the show date. Some breeders remove the spot feathers to ensure that they too will be firmly established in good time. This practice cannot be recommended for beginners because, on some occasions,the spot feathers do not regrow until some months later—if at all.

Cage training: To exhibit in the normal classes, a Budgerigar must be shown in a standard cage carrying an ivorine label issued by the parent body. These cages can be bought from one of the advertisers in a fancy newspaper or a local appliance stockist.

Whilst the birds are in the stock cage being prepared for exhibition, they can be run into a show cage and left there for a couple of hours daily. Seed should be in a layer covering the floor and drinking water provided in a plastic clip-on fount. (This is removed before sending the exhibit.)

Show-cage training, encouraging the bird to hop from perch to perch occasionally, using a judging stick or short piece of 8 mm

($^5/_{16}$ in) dowel rod will help steady it and prepare it for the judge's attentions.

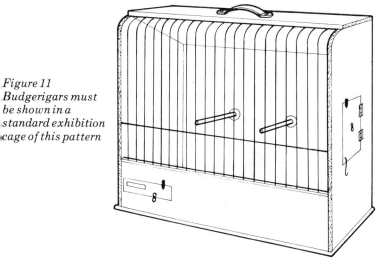

Figure 11
Budgerigars must
be shown in a
standard exhibition
cage of this pattern

Washing and spraying: A couple of weeks before the show, really grimy birds, especially the paler varieties, should be handwashed with a baby shampoo. This should be done in the morning so that the bird can be thoroughly dried out—in a hospital cage, on a radiator, or in front of a fire—before it goes to roost. Using three bowls of warm water, apply shampoo and water from the first one with an old shaving brush or soft toothbrush following the direction of the feathers. Rinse off in the second bowl and finally in the third. Wrap the bird loosely in a warm dry flannel—or similar—and leave it on the cage floor to dry. It will wriggle free later.

A daily spraying with warm water from a pressure spray for a week or so prior to the show, whether a bird has been shampooed or not, will encourage it to preen; this will clean the feathers making them lie smooth and shiny to the body, and promote alertness and physical condition. It is best to use rainwater.

Some breeders use ordinary tap water softened with a pinch of borax and sometimes add rose water to promote a sheen to the feathers. All spraying should be discontinued a couple of days before the show date. About this time, any surplus flecking on the mask should be carefully removed.

Hints on show procedure

Entry forms: Please remember, when filling in the entry form, that only current-year Budgerigars carrying the breeder's own close-coded ring issued through the parent body can be entered into 'Breeders Classes'. All other Budgerigars, whether young or adult, ringed or unringed, must be entered into the 'Any Age' or 'Adult' classes. Where no special class is scheduled for the particular colour or variety of the intended exhibit, the bird should be entered in the class for Any Other Colour (AOC) or Any Other Variety (AOV).

The exhibition cage: The cage labels will arrive a few days in advance of the show. Fix one of these to the centre of the wooden cage front. The cage should be cleaned thoroughly and about 1 cm (½ in) of the usual seed should be placed on the cage floor. Gently run the bird, preferably without handling, into the cage.

A common error, which can be avoided, is entering birds in the wrong classes or, at the last minute,running the birds into wrongly-labelled cages. A little extra care in this direction will avoid the entry being 'Wrong Classed' by the Judge with all the associated wasted effort. It only remains to take the exhibits along to the show hall at the prescribed time.

The cages in transit should be covered over with brown paper or a cloth covering or put in a box to avoid fright and draught. Make certain that there is sufficient ventilation in the cages.

Judging: This is not an easy task, especially if the birds are nervous and moving rapidly around their cages. This is why it is a good idea to accustom your bird to the exhibition cage well before the show. Standards have been established for all the accepted colours and varieties of Budgerigar and the judge awards points for particular features, e.g. condition, type, mask and spots, colour.

After the show: No bird can be removed from the show before the official lifting time or without the special permission of the show manager. Many shows provide a lifting card, showing the class and cage number of the exhibits to facilitate the checking-out from the show hall.

When the birds arrive home they should be returned to the stock cages for a couple of days to avoid chills.

A suitable tonic from the pet-shop or a few drops of compound syrup of hypophosphates from a chemist can be added to the drinking water at this time to promote a rapid return to high condition. Alternatively, a piece of millet spray can be offered which has previously been soaked overnight in a solution of 1 teaspoonful of Parishes' chemical food to 1 pint of water.

Many Budgerigar breeders gain great satisfaction from their hobby without ever entering a show, but most experience a competitive urge to measure their breeding skill against that of others. Not only do shows provide the arena for this competition, they also present an opportunity to compare notes with other breeders and gain further experience.

2
Canaries

Origins

The Canary (*Serinus canarius*) is said to have greatly impressed the Spanish conquistadores, who, when they landed in the Canary Islands in 1478, were enthralled by its melodious singing. Subsequently, these charming little birds were to find favour throughout Europe in the homes of the rich and the famous.

The Canary of today comes in a variety of sizes and colours but that which was popularised by the Spanish was about 10 cm (4 in) long and greenish yellow in colour. Records show that the Spanish were able to control the sales of canaries for over a century by retaining the females and disposing only of the male birds. However, in the sixteenth century, a galleon laden with Canaries was wrecked and many of the birds escaped to the island of Elba. The Italians, overjoyed at their good fortune, lost no time in breeding the escapees with the result that the Canary soon found its way to various parts of Europe and elsewhere, where it is still being bred today.

Choosing and buying your bird

Which breed of Canary to choose is often a problem for the novice. The best advice, if you are not prepared to take pot luck and answer the first advertisement or purchase whatever the pet-shop has on offer, is to visit a show advertised in *Cage and Aviary Birds* or *American Cage Bird Magazine*. There, you will be able not only to talk with breeders and exhibitors, but to select the variety which has the greatest appeal.

There is no 'best breed' for the newcomer but the Belgians, Scots Fancies and Crested Canaries are perhaps best avoided. Much skill is required in training the first two for the show bench and the head gear of the third needs much care and attention.

Among the best breeds for the beginner are the Border, Yorkshire and Norwich Canaries. The Border is the easiest to breed because there is no colour feeding, beyond the giving of marigold flowers or nasturtiums to improve the natural colour of exhibition birds. This is because the specialist clubs that look after the interests of this breed do not allow the birds to be colour fed.

Of course, if your main motivation for buying a Canary is to obtain an attractive *singing* bird, then the essential to remember is that *only male birds sing* and the pet-shop should be able to deal with your requirements. A little research before purchase usually protects a buyer from subsequent disappointment, should he or she later discover a variety they would have preferred. Before making a final decision, therefore, write for information to a specialist canary club, such as the British Border Fancy Canary Club, the International Border Fancy Canary Club or one of several others in the UK or USA which are listed under *Useful addresses*.

Figure 12 The Norwich Canary is an ideal breed for the novice

Make sure that you have heard the bird in song before purchase and do bear in mind that there is a slight difference in the melodies produced by different varieties. The Roller Canary, for instance, gives voice in a kind of trill whereas the Chopper Canary is said to sing 'in romantic vein'. Importantly, whichever variety of Canary you buy, make sure that it looks lively and is not sitting dejectedly on its perch, there is no discharge from eyes and nose and no greeny white droppings on the floor of the cage.

Figure 13 The Border Canary is one of the easiest types from which to breed. This is a clear buff cock

Accommodation

See that the cage is sufficiently large to allow complete comfort for your chosen bird. If the cage has small, round perches (which will be found in many wire cages) you should change them for perches made of soft, white wood such as spruce or larch, shaping them with a plane to roughly 1.25 cm (½ in) square and then taking off the sharp edges. Such perches are far more comfortable and help to prevent claw and leg troubles.

Site the cage in a light, airy position, free from draughts, where the temperature remains even. It should not be hung high up in the room above the level of the lights, where the atmosphere tends to become hot, stuffy and full of harmful fumes, nor should it be hung in a window where the sun's rays through the glass can prove harmful, causing overheating and irritation. It is a risk to keep pet birds in a room that is extremely warm by day and very cold at night. This tends to bring on soft moult.

Hygiene

The most convenient covering for the floor of the cage is a sand sheet, which makes for ease of cleaning and the utmost hygiene. Alternatively, a proprietary mixture of shell and sand, which has been treated, may be used. This also helps mastication besides acting as a tonic to the system. Grit in some form is essential to aid the digestion and is best given in a separate hopper. All hoppers should be kept scrupulously clean and should be thoroughly washed at least once a week or more frequently if necessary.

The cleaning of the cage should never be deferred for more than 3 days at the most. However careful you are about the cleanliness of the cage, it is often difficult to avoid the appearance of red mite; these pests are nocturnal in habit, but can be quickly banished by using an aerosol insecticide on the perches and cracks of the cage before sterilising the cage and contents by immersion in boiling water.

Feeding

Clean fresh water must be supplied daily for drinking and sufficient water must be given in one water container for bathing.

Seeds are the main feature in the diet of the majority of household pet birds, but to ensure obtaining seeds of the best quality and nutritional value, it is vital to choose a good standard canary mixture, containing a selection of the best and most suitable seeds in the correct proportions, cleaned by a process which frees it from all dust and foreign matter. In addition to seed, a little green food or fruit should be given every other day. Watercress, chickweed, seeding grasses, young leaves and seeding heads of the dandelion, milk thistle, ripe plantain stalk, lettuce and portions of the young inner leaves of cabbage or Brussels sprouts are all suitable. Always be sure that they are free from frost and, in the case of lettuce (unless its source is known), well washed and dried, as some lettuce that comes from overseas is treated with an insecticide which can prove harmful to pet birds. Fruit, such as apple, pear and banana, is a suitable substitute and, when this is not available, raw carrot may be given. Bread-and-milk is the main source of amino acids which are essential to good feather growth; it should be given two or three times a week. Glucose may be sprinkled on it to make it more palatable to the bird. Cuttlefish bone provides calcium and also helps to prevent excess growth of the beak.

Training

The Canary is a hardy little bird and easy to look after; also it very rarely bites. Nevertheless, once you have bought your pet home, do refrain from handling it until it has had a chance to settle down and get to know you; adopt, in fact the same familiarisation procedure outlined for the Budgerigar (p. 17).

First of all the bird's confidence must be gained. This is absolutely essential. The Canary must be handled without fuss or excitement and always spoken to quietly and soothingly. Always remember that a blustering loud voice, or a sudden, quick movement in the vicinity of the cage, will tend to frighten the bird; nothing will be achieved but the taming process will suffer a setback.

It is a good idea to place the bird's cage on a table and then to sit quietly close to it. At first, the bird is likely to crouch in a corner of the cage, scared by its new and unfamiliar surroundings. With patient persistence and gentle talking, you will gradually gain its confidence as it becomes accustomed to its new surroundings and the sound of your voice. Obviously, the bird should have only one teacher.

When you feel that the bird is no longer frightened by your presence, very gently insert your whole hand through the door of the cage with the forefinger extended. Do not withdraw the bird from the cage but lightly caress its head, talking to it quietly for a while. Subsequently, slight pressure of the forefinger against the bird's legs while it is standing on the perch will eventually persuade it to perch on your finger. Again, do not immediately attempt to withdraw the bird from the cage. Allow plenty of time for it to get used to this action. As its confidence grows, you will eventually be able to take the bird from the cage and bring it out into the room on the hand. In a surprisingly short time, it will familiarise itself with its surroundings and will happily perch on your shoulder.

Although most people like to let their bird free, do not imagine that it is *essential* for every pet bird to be given the freedom of the room. It is not. Indeed many experts express the view that these so called 'freedom lessons' reduce the lifespan of pet birds. On this view I cannot comment, but certainly there are many hazards, such as unguarded fires, open windows and doors, vases full of water and, in kitchens, pans full of boiling fat or water, all of which have regrettably featured in tragedies at some time or another. Provided that the cage is large enough (and it is important to allow for wing span), a bird will live quite contentedly within its confines if that is your wish.

Breeding

The breeding season commences in spring and lasts until July. It is unwise to begin breeding too early and many over-enthusiastic owners have regretted starting in February or early March. In the UK, at least, there are two good reasons for delaying the breeding season until late March or April. In the first place, in the winter, days are short and nights are long and the long interval between the last feed and the first feed next morning is bad for the young bird. Secondly,the dry east and northeast winds which are so prevalent early in the year affect the fertility of the male birds and have a prejudicial effect upon the young. Moreover, these winds dry and toughen the inner membrane of the shell so that the young have difficulty in breaking it when the time of hatching arrives.

When breeding Canaries one should make haste slowly. The best time of year to buy birds for breeding purposes is the autumn, to give them a while to settle down in their new home before it is time for breeding. It is unwise to buy birds, take them to a strange bird room and mate them straight away. The longer they are in the room which is to be their home, the more likely they are to breed well.

Special feeding

You will need to prepare your birds for breeding with some special feeding. The birds should be given as their staple food some well known proprietary canary mix and, for a month before pairing, a special breeding food.

If the birds are fed as recommended for several weeks, they should be in breeding condition from the middle of March onwards. Their fitness may be decided by watching their movements. If they are ready to breed, they will be flying from perch to perch in their cages, dancing on their perches, flapping their wings and calling to each other.

When these signs are observed, you may be assured that the birds are fit and that, if the middle of March has arrived, breeding operations may be commenced.

Special accommodation

If you decide to breed canaries on a large scale, you will need a bird room. You must consider the cages and other appliances which are necessary. Taking the breeding cage first, it is generally agreed that the best form is the plain box cage, i.e. a cage about 50 cm (25 in) long, 25 cm (10 in) deep from back to front and 40 – 45 cm (16 – 18 in) high. The top, back, sides and bottom are of wood and the front of wire. The door is in the middle of the front and the feeding and drinking holes are at either end.

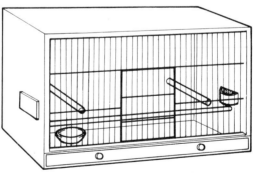

Figure 14 This breeding cage is suitable for Canaries and should be equipped with a nest pan, supported by a wire basket

There should be one perch running the length of the cage, close to the feeding holes, and two other perches higher up on the cross bar of the front. Some breeders fix only one top perch in the middle of the cage, but two are preferable as this prevents crowding when the young birds leave the nest.

The double cage, which follows virtually the same pattern as the single, is divided into two compartments by a wooden or wire slide. This enables the birds to be separated with the minimum of trouble. It is larger than the single cage, being about 90 cm (36 in) long, 25 cm (10 in) deep and 40—45 cm (16—18 in) high.

A nest pan should be supported from the back or side of the cage in a wire basket. A nest lining should be inserted in the pan. A little paste round the edges will keep the lining in position.

Breeding cages with all the necessary fittings—seed boxes, drinking glasses and troughs for soft food—are sold by the best bird-dealers and are regularly advertised in *Cage and Aviary Birds* and *American Cage Bird Magazine*. There is a diversity of opinion as to whether the cage bottom should have a false sliding bottom or tray, or a turn rail, fixed at the bottom of the front of the cage and worked on a pin. The sliding tray is generally to be preferred as this can be removed at any time, cleaned and put back again. With the turn rail, the cleaning is done by inserting a small scraper and drawing the refuse out into a dustpan or bucket.

Pairing

Beginners find it difficult to distinguish the sex of their birds, particularly when they are young. By paying very careful attention, you will notice that there is a difference between the voices of the male and female. The note of the cock is short and sharp while that of the hen is much longer and more decided. The cock is generally larger and more massive than the hen, bolder and more energetic in his movements and his action generally is quick and decisive. The head of the cock is usually longer as well. When the birds are fully grown, it is usually easier to determine the sex by examination of the vent: that of the hen is small and in the same straight line as the body, while that of the cock is more prominently developed.

The hen should be in her breeding cage some time before the cock is introduced to her. He should on no account be suddenly placed in the breeding cage with no preliminaries. If a single breeding cage is used, it is wise to place him in an open wire cage, which should be hung on the front of the breeding cage; the hen may then view her prospective mate from afar and gradually get used to his advances. The birds should be allowed to get used to each other gradually and, when they are seen to be friendly, talking to each other and feeding one another through the wires of the cages, the cock may be put in the hen's cage.

When birds are bought for the purpose of breeding they must be carefully fed for some time before being mated. It is as essential for the birds to become used to the food as it is for them to become used to the accommodation, which is another reason for buying them in advance. It is useless to expect to be successful in breeding young Canaries if the birds are not brought into fit condition before being mated.

Nesting and incubation

After a few days, a little nest material may be introduced in between the wires of the breeding cage. As soon as the birds are fit, they will be seen carrying this about the cage. Now is the time to introduce the nest pan and the remaining nest material.

In a day or so, the birds will be seen carrying the nesting material to the nest pan and the hen will be busy forming a nest. After a further few days, she will show signs of wanting to go to the nest and become slightly slower in her movements. Her abdomen will look fuller and, one morning when you enter the room, you will find her on the nest. As you approach the cage she will possibly fly off onto the perch and, on looking into the nest, you will discover an egg.

There is a possibility of your bird becoming eggbound and, if this occurs, she should be removed from the breeding cage and placed in a small cage, without a perch, but with a piece of flannel covering the cage floor. This cage should then be placed somewhere near a fire or stove so that the warmth will assist in the passing of the eggs. Let the bird remain by the fire for an hour or so after the eggs have passed and then return her to the breeding cage.

It is customary among the best breeders to remove the first three eggs each morning as they are laid, returning them on the fourth morning. This may be done by removing the nest from the cage, then lifting each egg with a teaspoon and placing it on a saucer containing bran or sawdust. Before returning the nest, some fanciers put a dummy egg into it. It is wise to use dummy eggs as they keep the hen quiet and prevent her from worrying about the eggs she has laid. Birds have nerves and it is not advisable to upset them.

On the fourteenth morning, the young Canaries may be expected, although in warm weather they often make their appearance on the evening of the thirteenth day after the parents began to incubate the eggs.

The question of bathing is important. Birds delight in using a bath but while the hen bird is sitting on her eggs, and until the young birds have passed the age of 3 weeks, a bath should not be given. At all other periods throughout the year, clean bathing water should be given every other day, except on very cold damp days in the winter. It should always be given early in the morning so that there is no fear of the birds standing on the perches at night with damp feathers. Regular use of the bath as indicated, winter or summer, will add much to the health and strength of the birds.

A word of warning—never fuss your bird. It is natural to be anxious when the young are about to hatch. Do not let your anxiety lead you to interfere with the nest. On the morning the young birds are expected, approach the cage with a piece of fresh green food. Place it in the wires of the cage and step back. The hen is almost certain to leave the nest. Then take a peep. Look, but do not handle.

From this point onwards, until the hen begins to think about her second family, keep the birds supplied with fresh clean water every day, renewing it twice, or even thrice, in hot weather. Green food soon withers and if this is given fresh several times a day, the old birds will appreciate it and will feed the young far better. Feed regularly and as often as possible. The fresher the food given, the better the birds will thrive. If any of the green food is pulled on the floor of the cage, pick it up and throw it away. Green food that is trampled on the floor of the cage soon goes bad and decomposes. This is not good for the bird. The need for fresh green food at frequent intervals cannot be emphasised too strongly. Damaged, dirty green food, soiled by excreta, if eaten, creates gas in young birds, upsetting the digestive organs and causing inflammation of the bowels. Prevention is better than cure.

Care of young birds

When the young are nearing the age of 3 weeks, the hen will begin to think about her second nest. This is the time for you to give her another nest pan and a little fresh nest material. Do not wait until the hen is too forward. Give the new nest pan and nest material as soon as she shows signs of leaving her young. It will not cause her to lay before her time, but it will prevent her from plucking the young. This she will certainly do unless you give her fresh nesting material.

When she goes to nest a second time, remove the eggs in the same manner as before. Do not worry about the young in the first nest. Even though the hen is thinking about her second family, she will not neglect the first as long as you keep her regularly fed with fresh greens and soft foods. Indeed, when she settles down to incubate the second clutch, the cock bird will attend to the feeding of the young.

Feeding: There are sometimes severe losses of young Canaries at about 6 weeks of age due to inflammation of the bowels, caused through eating hard seed too early. You should therefore ensure that they have a supply of natural food until they can satisfactorily manage the seed. Great care must be taken to see that they never go hungry. It is best to continue to give bread and milk until they are eating seed and it is very necessary to see that they do not get too much water. During this period, the water vessel is best given three times a day, for just long enough for them to drink, and then taken away again. If the birds appear to be sick at this age, it is as well to put a dusting of bismuth carbonate on their food until they have recovered.

The second batch of nestlings should be given exactly the same treatment as the first.

Hygiene: Remember that cleanliness is essential for success in Canary breeding so keep all feeding and drinking vessels scrupulously clean. It is wise to scald them out every morning. Remove the tray of the breeding cage and of any other cages that are used once a week. Clean thoroughly and give the floor a fresh covering of bird sand. The sand not only absorbs the moisture from the excreta but also supplies the grit necessary for breaking down the food.

Breeders may be troubled with red mite in the nest or breeding cage and this parasite should be exterminated immediately. If it is noticed, make a new nest for the young and place it in a new cage. Burn the infested nest and wash the original cage thoroughly in hot water, soap and a good disinfectant.

A nest of strong, healthy young create a lot of excreta, but do not worry about the dirty nest. For the first week, the hen will clean much of this away. On the eighth day, give the young a clean nest pan and a new nest lining.

When you take the young from the cage in the nest pan do the changing outside of the cage. Lift the nest pan from the hanger, keeping your hand over the top of the nest to prevent the young birds from falling out. Place the nest pan on a table or chair, remove the young quickly from it, put them in a new one and return it at once.

The dirty nest pan should be removed from the bird room immediately and thoroughly cleansed in a pan of hot water containing some soda.

Fledging: By the end of the month, the young birds will be able to feed themselves and they may then be removed from the breeding cage into either a breeding cage or a flight cage. The former is best because they will be accustomed to the fittings. They can go into a flight cage later when they are strong on the wing. Continue to give breeding food and all the rest of the attention you have been giving them, making no change in their diet nor in seeing to their needs. When they are 6 weeks old, you may reduce the amount of breeding food to one feed a day but supplement it with a standard canary mixture. This will give them all the nutrition they need.

Breeding Canary mules

Canary mules are the offspring of a cross between a Canary and a British or foreign finch. The fascination which attends mule breeding is undoubtedly due to the great element of chance involved. One never knows what to expect in mule breeding whereas, in the breeding of any type of Canary, e.g. two Norwich, the young will always be Norwich and nothing else. Breeding canaries is generally successful and those who practise mule breeding do get fertile eggs and progeny in most cases. Years ago, mules between Canaries and Goldfinches and Linnets were the only ones that were at all common. Then mules

Figure 15 A Canary-Bullfinch mule—1974 Champion

between Canaries and Siskins became more frequently seen.

At one time Canary-Redpoll and Canary-Bullfinch mules were thought to be impossible but they have now been accomplished.

Such crosses as the Goldfinch-Canary, Siskin-Canary, Linnet-Canary and Greenfinch-Canary are also very common, but the Bullfinch-Canary is still a rarity.

The management of Canaries and Finches, when used for breeding mules, is similar to that followed in the breeding of Canaries. Many mules have been produced by amateurs with no knowledge whatsoever of bird management but success is more likely to be achieved when proper preparation is made than when chance governs the whole thing.

In the first place, a double breeding cage should be used, i.e. a cage 86—92 cm (34—36 in) long, 25 cm (10 in) deep and 40—45 cm (16—18 in) high. There is a diversity of opinion as to the covering of the cage floor. Some breeders use only sand, as when breeding Canaries, while others cover the bottom of all mating cages with material such as rice hulls, wheat hulls, chaff, moss and short lengths of dried grass, the idea being to make the surroundings more natural. Success has been

Figure 16 A Canary-Greenfinch mule

achieved whatever has been used and bird breeders may please themselves what they adopt. If one method does not succeed another can be tried.

One of the great essentials to success in breeding Canary mules is to have all the birds perfectly tame. This may be best achieved by keeping the different pairs each in their own separate breeding cages from the moulting season of one year to the breeding season of the next. Then the more they are fussed and played with the more likely they are to be quiet and domesticated when the time for breeding approaches.

Finches are not usually ready for breeding as early in the year as Canaries and, therefore, it is wise not to give the muling birds nest pans or nesting material until about the middle of April. Those who breed Canary mules regularly often run hen Canaries with a cock Canary first and take one brood of young Canaries from them before introducing the hens to a Finch. If this is not done the cock Finch and hen Canary should each be kept in its own compartment of the breeding cage from January onwards; the wire slide dividing the cage should be kept in position so that the birds may see and talk to each other and do their courting through the wire.

When breeding Goldfinch-Canary mules, the Goldfinch must never have the run of the breeding cage. When the hen Canary looks as though she is ready to breed, the slide should be removed and the Goldfinch allowed in the hen's compartment during the latter part of the day. If they pair up successfully, the Goldfinch may be removed and a nest pan and some nesting material given to the Canary hen so that she may proceed to build her nest.

The Finch may be allowed in the cage each day for a short time and then be shut off into his own compartment. When the eggs are laid, they should be removed in the way described on p. 43 and the Finch should not be allowed in the hen's compartment until after the egg has been removed each morning. After the fourth egg has been laid he should be removed and the cage should be divided with the wooden slide instead of the wire. This is imperative when a Goldfinch or Greenfinch is used as they have a nasty habit of breaking the eggs. Sometimes, other Finches also break the eggs but, as a rule, cock Linnets and Siskins may be left with their mates as they make equally good parents as cock Canaries.

The general feeding directions given in the section on breeding Canaries may be followed in the case of mules, but the staple food should be a proprietary Canary mix.

Exhibiting

The Fancy

Cage bird shows were discussed at some length on p. 27 and, to avoid duplicating information, I would suggest that the reader also studies the sections on *Exhibiting* in other chapters. As I have said, the time is likely to come when the owner of a pet bird or, indeed, a new breeder, will wish to enter his or her stock in a show to see how it stands up to the birds of other exhibitors. It is also likely that, before this, you will have become acquainted with other members of the Canary Fancy through joining a local caged bird club or becoming a member of a specialist club such as the British Roller Canary Association, the Canary Colour Breeders Association (which, incidentally, although British-based, has international membership of more than 500 members) or, in the USA, perhaps the American Border Fancy Canary Club, the American Norwich Society, the Yorkshire Canary Club of America or one of several others. There is even an American Singers Club formed expressly for the raising and showing of Canaries bred for beautiful song and judged almost solely on this quality. Please note that these are a fraction of the available clubs and societies.

Figure 17 A Clear-capped Gold Lizard Canary cock

There are, for example, two societies for the Roller Canary in the UK alone: the National Roller Canary Society, which has clubs and members mainly in the Midlands and the south, and the British Roller Canary Association, whose clubs are located mainly in the Lancashire and Yorkshire area. Membership of both Associations is by joining one of the member clubs. These dedicated bodies specialise in the *song* of the Roller Canary and do not hold shows for type or colour.

The history of the Roller Canary and its song is a particularly interesting one. Their fame as vocalists began in St Andreasburgh in the Hartz Mountains of Germany, where it was discovered that the birds had a great gift of mimicry. This gift was exploited by the early fanciers (in about 1650) by using hand-operated water-machines, which produced rolling, bubbling water sounds, which the birds absorbed into their repertoire, thereby becoming known as 'Water Slagers'. The song was further improved by using nightingales as tutors, until the Hartz Mountain Roller Canaries developed a world-wide reputation as singers.

Details of shows can be located through the advertisement columns of club magazines and in *Cage and Aviary Birds* or *American Cage Bird Magazine*. All specialist clubs have an official standard of excellence for their variety and it is by this standard that the Canaries are judged.

Shows and patronage
Basically there are only two types of shows in the Canary Fancy, and also two stages, these being a club and open show and champion and novice status.

Obviously before exhibiting at a club show one has to be a member of the relevant society, a fact which qualifies the new member/exhibitor to show as a novice. A novice becomes a champion once he/she has won three classes of no less than eight exhibits, shown by at least three exhibitors.

An interesting point is, that if the new breeder/exhibitor decides to join several clubs, he/she can continue showing as a novice for the remainder of the show season, but in the following year must exhibit as a champion at all the clubs unless precluded from doing so by a specific rule.

Club show wins do not count at open shows so it is not unusual for club champions of long standing to continue exhibiting as novices at a number of open shows. The open show, unlike the club member's show, is open to anyone who wishes to enter an exhibit.

Rules at such shows vary but, as with a club show, it is generally accepted that, having won three first prizes in classes with no less than eight exhibitors, the entrant becomes a champion but, again, may continue to show in novice classes for the remainder of that particular season. Unlike the procedure in canine and other fancies, it is a case of once a champion always a champion and the exhibitor cannot begin again at novice stage showing another Canary.

A number of specialist clubs run patronage to open shows at which special prizes are offered and some associations such as the Canary Colour Breeders Association, promote their own all colour canary shows, where there are many trophies up for competition. The latter Association is but one which has a scheme for training judges, in this case, culminating in a trainee judge of the year competition.

3
Zebra Finches

Origins

Since they were first imported from Australia, Zebra Finches (*Taeniopygia guttata castanotis*) have been the favourite aviary birds of a great many people due, mainly, to their disarming ways, the ease with which they breed and their ability to face varied weather conditions. There are, it must be emphasised, a great number of other Finch varieties, but some of these are very small and immense care has to be taken lest they slip through the food containers in their cages.

In 1952, keepers and breeders of Zebra Finches in the UK were becoming so numerous that a few of the most keen banded together and formed a specialist society for the variety's advancement.

At about this time, mutations among Finches had begun to appear and this greatly enhanced their popularity with both exhibitors and aviary keepers. A further point in their favour was their ability to make excellent foster parents for some of the rarer foreign birds which was a great encouragement to breeders generally to keep them.

It would be true to say that, about 30 years ago, only the Normal (Grey) Zebra Finch was generally available from aviaries. These specimens were freely imported from Australia and consisted of a number of subspecies which have been interbred to give the present-day varieties. This accounts for the small changes in depth of colour and markings that are seen today. Without doubt, the appearance of mutations increased the interest of fanciers in producing Zebra Finches and adding to the number of possible combinations. There is now available a considerable variety of these little birds.

Figure 18 A Normal (Grey) Zebra Finch cock

Choosing and buying your bird

At present, there are some eight distinct colour forms of Zebra Finches and also combinations of some of these colour forms, e.g. Normal Grey, White Albino, Chestnut-flanked White, Fawn, Silver, Cream, Pied, Penguin, Yellow-beaked and Crested.

If you intend to keep Zebra Finches, it would certainly help to join the Zebra Finch Society. At the time of writing, this Society has a membership of over 1500 and it is unfailingly helpful both in assisting newcomers and in getting deserved recognition for the breed. Indeed, because Zebra Finches all breed so well in captivity, with no introduction of any wild coarse stock, the Zebra Finch Society, in 1958, proclaimed to the bird fancy generally that these Finches were fully domesticated birds and could no longer be classed as foreign in the UK. This decision was met with considerable approval and helped in gaining even more popularity for the Zebra Finch.

With its growing popularity, you should have little difficulty in buying the specimens you want, by looking through the advertisement columns of *Cage and Aviary Birds* or *American Cage Bird Magazine*, enquiring of your local pet-shop owner or writing to one of the addresses at the end of this book.

Figure 19 A Chestnut-flanked White Zebra Finch cock

Accommodation

The Zebra Finch is a hardy little bird which is easy to keep and breeds readily in cages.

Cages should be as long as possible, about 75×30 cm (30×12 in) in area and 45 cm (18 in) high. This size should accommodate one breeding pair and up to ten non-breeding birds. The front should have a large door (that designed for a Budgerigar should be satisfactory).

Figure 20 The Zebra Finch is a small bird and a cage like this will accommodate up to ten birds

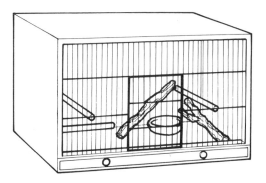

The perches should be of varying thicknesses, made either from dowelling or natural branches. Seed, water and grit dishes should be placed on the floor but not under perches. The cage may be painted with emulsion but this must be quite dry before the birds are introduced.

Zebra Finches, if kept indoors, require no extra heat in the winter as the normal house temperature is adequate. They are, however, susceptible to draughts, particularly as they are regular bathers and, when wet, a draught can be lethal!

Hygiene

As with all birds, cleanliness is imperative and the cage floor and perches must be cleaned regularly (at least twice a week). Food and water dishes should be cleaned daily, all husks blown off and fresh seed added.Clean water must be given daily and green stuff should be fed in small quantities each day, preferably in a rack off the floor.

Bird rooms

If you have a bird room, it should be draught-proof, damp-proof and vermin-proof. Indeed, the Zebra Finch Society has emphasised that, if mice are present in a bird room, they will certainly contaminate the food and also frighten the birds, usually with disastrous consequences. Zebra Finches are not happy in damp, draughty surroundings and such conditions will only impair their general fitness and health.

Whether or not heating will be required in your bird room depends on where you live, but any source of heating *must* be safe. Heaters which operate by burning solid or liquid fuel often give off fumes which are deadly to birds and tubular electric heaters controlled by a thermostat are probably the safest form of heating available. Supplementary lighting is usually necessary and electric lighting, controlled by dimmers or a time clock, is almost universally used. Secure locks should be fitted to all bird rooms as even unwitting intruders can do a great deal of damage to your stock and with very little effort.

Feeding

The basic diet consists of *Panicum* millet but other seeds can also be given, e.g. white millet, small canary seed, rape or niger. Millet sprays are a great favourite.

Soft food, such as bread and milk made crumbly moist, insects, and patent foods as used for canaries may also be given in small quantities but should be removed before they become stale. While breeding, birds will tend to eat more of these foods than at other times.

A regular supply of green food is necessary. Seeding heads of meadow grasses, rye grass and chickweed are excellent. Zebra Finches will also eat chickweed, shepherd's purse, plantains, sow thistles, spinach and dandelions. Sprouted seeds are also much appreciated.

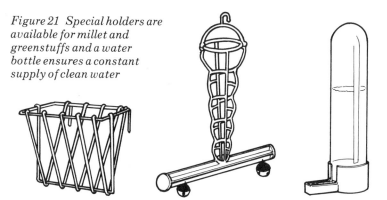

Figure 21 Special holders are available for millet and greenstuffs and a water bottle ensures a constant supply of clean water

Mixed grit is essential for their well-being. Cuttlefishbone supplies minerals and helps in keeping the beaks the correct length. Mineral blocks may also be used. Dried crushed eggshells are a useful source of minerals and old mortar an excellent source of calcium. Seed supplements in the form of condition seed and niger seed can be given with beneficial effect, although some individual birds seem to prefer their standard seed diet. A plentiful supply of grit and mineral should always be available to *all* birds. This is essential to digestion as well as general wellbeing. Fresh water must be given daily and, although Zebra Finches are not prolific drinkers, most *are* fanatical bathers. During the breeding season some form of rearing food should be given and there are many of these preparations available.

Breeding

To ensure satisfactory breeding, birds must be maintained in good condition. They should be active, bright-eyed and chase each other about the cage. You will observe the cock stretch its neck and let forth a chirp while the hen, carrying nesting material, looks for a suitable nesting site.

Once the birds are in this lively state, you can introduce a nesting box or basket, which should be at least two-thirds full of grass and some nesting material, such as soft, dried grass and feathers. It is wise (certainly in the UK) to delay the commencement of breeding until at least late February or March.

Figure 22 A wicker nesting basket, lined with grass, is ideal for Zebra Finches

Special accommodation

Ideally, breeding cages should be 60×40 cm (24×15 in) in area and 40 cm (15 in) high and fitted with budgerigar-type fronts. They should have two perches and a nest box, positioned suitably inside, ready for the introduction of the pair.

The nest boxes mentioned in the Silver Jubilee book of the Zebra Finch Society are 15×15×15 cm (6×6×6 in), with a removable lid and a half open front. They should always be half filled with nesting material, roughly fashioned into a nest, before being placed inside the breeding cage. Extra nesting material should be available on the cage floor and the surplus should be removed as soon as the first egg is laid.

Figure 23 Alternatively, a nest box with half-open front and removable lid will encourage your birds to lay

Nesting and incubation

Most pairs take to their nest box straight away; the odd couple may not be so keen. Sometimes, however, their interest may be rekindled by removing the box or placing it in a different position in the cage.

Usually the first eggs are laid a week after pairing. If the birds lay immediately, their eggs will not be fertile. Indeed, even when eggs are laid after the correct interval, it is still advisable to check on their fertility by conducting the following simple test. Hold the egg up to a light bulb and, if you can see red, vein-like structures, it is fertile. If, however, the eggs appear clear, they are not fertile and the clutch should be taken away and the pair allowed to lay again.

Once the nest is constructed and the eggs have been laid, all nesting material should be removed. This is because some birds will continue building what are called 'sandwich' nests, thereby covering the eggs.

The usual clutch is five, incubation commencing after the laying of the second or third egg. The eggs take 12 days to hatch, with both parents incubating and, within 16−18 days, the youngsters should be ready to vacate the nest.

Care of young birds

Feeding: Most pairs will rear their young on brown bread soaked in milk and their normal seed diet. Some pairs may prefer to feed their young almost wholly on brown bread soaked in milk while others will feed them mainly on seed. The most important thing is that they are well fed. Youngsters which always have half empty crops rarely develop into good show specimens.

Fledging: At 4 weeks of age, most young will be self-supporting but this can prove a difficult period with Zebra Finches. This is because some parent birds are inclined to stop feeding their young before they are able to fend adequately for themselves.

If one of the parents is removed to another cage, the remaining bird may continue to feed the young but this is the exception rather than the rule. The young should be left with their parents until they are 5 weeks old if possible.

Sometimes parents will chase and chivvy their young as soon as they are self-supporting and, in such cases, it is as well to remove the little ones as soon as possible.

When first removed, youngsters should be placed in a cage where they can become accustomed to being on their own without interference from older and bigger Zebra Finches. Once they appear to be coping well on their own, they can be transferred to larger flight cages, along with the other, current-year youngsters. It is sensible to sex the fledglings and house them separately as some may be sufficiently precocious to start breeding as early as 3 months of age.

Exhibiting your bird

For many Zebra Finch fanciers, the object of the breeding season is to produce matched pairs of birds suitable for exhibition purposes. To do this, any stock used must be of excellent quality. You cannot produce good show birds from poor stock.

In other areas of the bird Fancy, exhibits are staged singly but in the Zebra Finch Fancy, birds are shown in pairs of matching colour. It is important that both members of the pair should match visually as regards type, shape, colour, shade and size, and that both members of the pair should be good examples of their particular colour.

The shape, or type, of the bird is most important, as it is the bird's outline which makes it instantly recognisable as a member of its species and/or variety.

The term 'cobby', as used in the standard for Zebra Finches, refers

Figure 24 A Crested Normal Zebra Finch cock

to birds of good substance, showing good depth and width of body, well rounded in the head, carrying the wings neatly to the root of the tail and not showing any specific type faults.

Specific type faults include drooping tails, pinched necks, hollow beaks, heavy beaks, square chests, flat heads, crossed wings, drooping wings etc. All these features detract from the general appearance of the birds; they should be avoided in stock birds and it should be noted that they will be penalised in show birds.

The 'type' for all colours of Zebra Finches should be the same but there are colours noted for being generally associated with good type and others associated with poorer type. Therefore, to be fair to all colours, judges tend to assess the type of any bird by comparing it with other examples of its own colour.

Obviously all birds need to be up to a certain standard, regardless of colour, but to expect the newer varieties to be instantly as good as those longer established would really be too optimistic. When Zebra Finches have been bred in captivity for as long as some of the older established varieties of cage birds, no doubt all colours will be of very similar types. Meanwhile, if allowance is not made for some colours, it would only serve to discourage the development of the newer varieties, thereby limiting the expansion of the Fancy.

Figure 25 A Fawn Zebra Finch cock

Markings on Zebra Finches are most important in exhibition birds and, where applicable, must be clear and distinct. The standard lays down clearly what is required and it is not acceptable to ignore faults in markings, even if the birds on show are outstanding in other respects. Any concession would lead to the eventual destruction of the marking pattern, a feature which attracted many hobbyists to the Zebra Finch Fancy in the first place.

The colour of Zebra Finches does, of course, vary from variety to variety but attention must be paid to the colour standards laid down by the Zebra Finch Society; specific notes on this can be gleaned from the Society's publications.

The desired size of birds is a favourite conversational topic but while size adds impact to birds on show, other features must not be neglected by exhibitors. All things being equal a good big one will generally beat a good little one, but conversely a bad big one should on no account beat a good little one.

Feather texture tends to be one of the most important factors in determining the visual size of birds, and buffs appear larger then yellows. While the difference between buffs and yellows in Zebra Finches is not particularly noticeable, however, there are many individual birds which are obviously either buffs or yellows. A common trap is to dispose of all yellows because they appear smaller and to breed only from buffs. This leads to the deterioration of colour and the production of birds which are too coarsely feathered.

The condition of the show bench exhibit is vitally important. After all, if condition were not taken into account there would be no reward for the fancier who had taken endless trouble to prepare and present his bird(s) correctly.

The Fancy
Writing in the Silver Jubilee book of the Zebra Finch Society, John A. W. Prior, its hardworking Honorary General Secretary, states with pride that, since its formation in 1952, the Zebra Finch Society has grown to become, by its Jubilee year, one of the largest international specialist societies in the bird Fancy.

Zebra Finches are traditionally regarded by most bird fanciers as an easy starter for those entering the foreign bird fancy, but over the years many fanciers have become devoted to the Zebra Finch in its own right, recognising its true value and the challenge it offers in mutation breeding and exhibition.

Mentioning that, in 25 years, 5247 members had passed through the Society's books, Mr Prior remarked that there was also the 'hidden' population—those who have kept or still keep Zebra Finches but have never entered membership of the Society. Indeed a Society census in 1974 showed that only one in three Zebra Finch owners and breeders belonged to the Society. The two-thirds majority recognise the Zebra Finch only as a friendly colourful little bird which they keep in their aviary. On this basis, and noting the fact that only half of the Zebra Finch Society members purchase rings, well over 100 000 finches must be bred in the UK each year.

On the exhibition side, the Zebra Finch Society continually appraises the position and alters its show classification to meet the demands of new mutations which have been recognised.

Patronage is awarded to over 150 open shows each year. A panel of judges covers all parts of the UK and is reviewed by the committee annually so that the highest possible standard is maintained. There is also an annual club show.

The Zebra Finch Society is supported by area societies in Scotland, the Scottish and northern counties, Yorkshire, the Midlands, East Anglia, the west of England and Kent; each accepts and maintains the parent society's rules, show classifications and standards. The Society co-exists with groups in the USA, Canada, Australia, New Zealand, France, Italy, Denmark, West Germany, Belgium, Holland and Sweden. Further information, details of membership and a copy of the latest newsletter can be obtained from the Secretary of the Zebra Finch Society.

Shows

According to the Society's rules, judges must observe the show and colour standards and birds can only be shown at patronage shows in true pairs, i.e. a cock and hen. A pair must always consist of two birds of the same mutation. No awards can be given unless the birds are in perfect show condition. Missing, ragged or soiled feathers and missing claws or toes consititute show faults. Type should be bold throughout and 'cobby', giving the birds a look of substance, and the wings should be evenly carried towards the tail.

The cocks should bear the following markings: distinct and clear-cut chest bar, not less than 3 mm (⅛ in) wide and of even width throughout; prominent side flankings extending from the wing butts to the end of the rump, decorated with round, clearly defined, white spots; coral red beak; deep pink feet and legs. All markings should be clear and distinct. The hen should be similarly marked but without the cheek patches, chest bar and side flankings; the beak should be a paler shade of red. Male markings on the hen are a definite show fault. For many Zebra Finch fanciers, the object of the breeding season is to produce matched pairs of birds suitable for exhibition purposes.

It is a rule of the Society that all pairs of birds entered as breeders and nominated BBE (Bred By Exhibitor) have to carry the closed, coded, current-year-dated rings of the breeder, purchased through the Zebra Finch Society, and be exhibited by that breeder. This is just one of the fifteen reasonable show rules laid down by the Zebra Finch Society.

Particulars of shows are given in both *Cage and Aviary Birds* and *American Cage Bird Magazine*.

Judging: In the case of the Zebra Finch Fancy, if you are a champion exhibitor of one year's standing and wish to be considered for the judges' panel, an application form may be obtained from the general secretary. Applications are considered at the appropriate committee meeting.

Patronage: Clubs can apply for open show patronage by writing to the patronage secretary, who is always pleased to supply application forms, on receipt of a stamped addressed envelope. Such forms have to be returned by the 31st March every year. Societies receiving patronage must agree to open the Zebra Finch classes to all Zebra Finch Society members wanting to exhibit.

The Society grants 3 types of patronage, support patronage (3 rosettes), full patronage (5 rosettes), area club show and Scottish club show (5 rosettes).

4
Parrots

Origins

The Parrot family is a very large one and is widely distributed throughout the tropical and sub-tropical regions of the world. Its members include Owl Parrots, Lories and Lorikeets, Pygmy Parrots, Cockatoos and the more familiar Parrots—Amazons and other short-tailed species, and Parrakeets, Lovebirds, Macaws and Parrotlets.

Parrots were kept by the Romans both for food and as pets and those which talked were often housed in sumptuous cages of silver. Centuries ago in India, they were regarded as sacred because of their ability to mimic human speech.

Parrots were brought to Spain by Columbus in 1493 and, by 1505, they had also been brought to the UK. Trading in Asiatic Parrots began in 1506, when the Portuguese took Ceylon and, soon after, the trade in South American Parrots—the Macaws and Amazons—began.

If you want a talking bird remember that the Parrot, although it will develop a considerable vocabulary, cannot reproduce the tone of a speaker's voice as the Mynah can. Also it is much more self-conscious, and is often reluctant to talk in front of strangers. Nevertheless, it is by far the most beautiful.

Choosing and buying your bird

If you intend to keep your Parrot in a cage, it is advisable to choose one of the short-tailed species. Four of the more commonly available are: the Cockatiel, the Blue-fronted Amazon, the Senegal and the

African Grey. There are, of course, other varieties which may take your fancy, but it is wise to seek advice from the Parrot Society or a respected dealer, before buying your chosen bird, on its care and handling and whether or not it can be taught to talk if this is your wish.

Many of the species most suitable as household pets are taken from the nest at an early age and hand-reared. Such birds are tame and confiding, allow themselves to be handled and, indeed, may have already started to talk.

Occasionally, adult birds are trapped for export. These seldom become tame and will retreat into a corner of the cage when approached. Dealers are generally anxious to get rid of such birds, so do not be tempted to buy birds at exceptionally low prices.

A tame healthy Parrot will sit boldly on its perch, its feathers bright and glossy and a bold inquisitive expression in its eyes. A bird with ruffled feathers, and partly closed eyes or its head under its wing with *both* feet on the perch is usually sick.

The Cockatiel (*Nymphicus hollandicus*), which comes from Australia, is particularly suitable for the newcomer to Parrot-keeping. It is very docile and makes an excellent personal pet. Should you have an aviary, it will co-exist happily with Finches, Doves and other small birds, even tiny Waxbills. It is hardy, seldom falls sick and is hardly ever bothered by moulting. As a cage pet it can be rather noisy but its confiding affectionate manner amply compensates for this. When cage-bred some *males* will learn to talk.

The adult male is grey with a white band extending from the shoulders over the greater wing coverts. The face and crest are primrose yellow and there is a brick-red patch on each cheek. The beak, legs and feet are grey. The female is duller in colour; the markings on the face are much reduced and the underside of the tail feathers is barred with yellow. The Cockatiel is fairly small for a Parrot, about 33 cm (13 in) long, nearly half of which is tail.

The Blue-fronted Amazon (*Amazona aestiva aestiva*) also makes an excellent cage pet. If you acquire a young bird and allow it to come into contact only with human beings, it will quickly become tame and, in time, it will become a clever mimic and an excellent talker. It can be rather noisy early in the mornings but its chatter will provide a great deal of amusement and pleasure.

Opposite: *Figure 26   The Cockatiel is an excellent first bird for the novice Parrot-keeper*

This bird is a native of Argentina, Brazil, Bolivia, and Paraguay. Both sexes are grass green generally with lighter underparts. The crown and the sides of the head, and the throat, are yellow and the forehead is blue. There is a lot of individual variation in the proportions of yellow and blue. The shoulders are scarlet, less prominently so in the hen, and so are the third and fourth flight feathers. The first and second flight feathers are blue. The green tail is washed with scarlet in the centre. The eyes are orange, the beak is blackish, and the legs and feet are grey. It is slightly bigger than the Cockatiel, about 38 cm (15 in) long.

Figure 27 The colourful Blue-fronted Amazon Parrot from South America is an excellent talker

The Senegal Parrot (*Poicephalus senegalus senegalus*) is found in West Africa from Senegal to Guinea-Bissau and first came to the UK in 1504, arousing considerable interest. Young birds become very tame and playful but, although they can learn to whistle tunes and mimic sounds, they show little talent for talking. Older birds are quite untameable and tend to remain shy and rather spiteful.

The male is green, darkest on the wings and tail, with a darkish grey head, paler and more silvery on the cheeks, and orange-yellow on the lower breast and abdomen. The beak is blackish and, in the adult, the iris of the eye is straw-coloured (grey in the juvenile). The tail is short-ish and the wings are noticeably long so that the tips reach the tail. The bird is just over 23 cm (9 in) long. The female is similar but less massive in appearance.

Figure 28 The Senegal Parrot makes an affectionate pet but has little talent for talking

The African Grey (*Psittacus erithacus erithacus*) has always been regarded as the most talented mimic and talker. It is highly intelligent and is capable of developing a considerable vocabulary. It will develop a great affection for its owner although it will merely tolerate other people. Occasionally you may find one with a spiteful or treacherous temperament.

The bird is generally grey but the margins of the head and neck feathers and the rump are very pale. The tail and coverts are dark scarlet in the juvenile but become brighter with age. The beak is black and the feet are dark grey. Bare white skin surrounds the eye. The iris is dark grey in young birds but yellow in adults. From beak to tail-tip, the bird is about 33 cm (13 in) long.

Figure 29 The most talented mimic is the African Grey Parrot

Accommodation

Most members of the Parrot family are very active in the wild and are very strong flyers. They are also very intelligent and inquisitive by nature. These factors must be taken into consideration when housing your bird.

Parrots adapt well to cage life but require regular exercise and, generally, company—either of their owner or another bird. It is important to prevent boredom, which is the prime cause of feather-plucking. Parrots are very prone to this habit. Should it be due to an infestation of skin or feather parasites, the feathers should be treated with an insecticidal spray or powder specifically prepared for birds. The cage, food containers, perches and trays should be thoroughly disinfected at the same time.

The standard all-wire Parrot cage is suitable for most birds but it must be large enough for your bird to stretch its wings fully. It should be of strong construction with an escape-proof catch on the door as Parrots are very ingenious. The cage should have a deep tray with a layer of dry sand or peat to absorb the droppings and discarded food.

The cage should be positioned about 1 m (3 ft) above the floor, against a wall, away from draughts and facing towards the light. It should not be left in direct sunlight for any length of time, however.

Figure 30 The standard all-wire cage is suitable for most Parrots

Accessories

Large, stout food and water containers made of easily cleanable material should be easily removable from the outside of the cage. There should be at least two perches, about 2.5 cm (1 in) in diameter—varying slightly to exercise the feet—so that your bird can hop from one to the other.

In a large cage, a swing may be hung from the top of the cage. A considerate owner will also supply a wooden cotton reel or a small bunch of twigs on which the bird can exercise its beak. A separate climbing pole, about 120 cm (48 in) high with a 46 cm (18 in) cross-bar may be provided on which the bird can perch when it is exercising outside its cage. Alternatively a perch may be provided on top of the cage.

The plumage of birds kept in cages tends to become dull and lifeless and it is often not practical to provide bathing facilities. A regular spray with tepid water will help overcome these problems.

Figure 31 A climbing-pole such as this will provide your Parrot with amusement and somewhere to perch when out of its cage

Feeding

The staple diet for the African Grey and the Amazon should consist of a 1 part sunflower seed and 2 parts budgerigar mixture. Once or twice a week a teaspoonful of either clipped oats, hemp seed, buck wheat or maize can be added for variety. Peanuts in the shell are relished; about five or six a day is enough. A daily ration of green food and/or fruit is advisable. The following are suggested, depending on your pet's preference and availability; grapes, bananas, oranges, apples, pears or any other fruit or berries in season. Root vegetables such as turnip, carrot, parsnip and the ribs of cabbage-type greens, spinach and sea-kale will also be taken. Some birds will eat the leaves of lettuce and other greens.

It is essential that fresh water is given daily, and grit to aid digestion and an adequate intake of minerals.

In addition to the staple diet, titbits can be given, such as dry toast with jam or honey, plain biscuit, boiled potato, rice or maize. Egg yolk, either soft or hard-boiled, may be given very occasionally. Too many titbits and table scraps are not advisable. A little brown bread made crumbly moist with milk may be given once a week as this supplies certain amino acids which are essential for good feather growth. Under no circumstances should left-overs from the table be given, as these are invariably salty, over seasoned and fatty.

The Cockatiel, in the wild, feeds on the seeds of native grasses. In captivity, a proprietary Budgerigar seed will serve as a staple diet, with the addition of millet spray, sunflower seed, sweet apple, raw carrot, seedling grasses and ripe grapes. A few oats should be given as well every few days.

When rearing nestlings, it is helpful to give the oats either as grain or when the young oats are green and plump. In addition, a rearing food, made crumbly moist with cold water and mixed with plenty of finely chopped green food, is useful.

Most imported Senegals have been fed on soft boiled white maize and have to be gradually weaned on to a normal diet of Parrot food and monkey nuts. The weaning period is sometimes a difficult one and must not be hurried; once successfully acclimatised they can even be safely wintered in an unheated aviary. Senegals, like all Parrots, should be given plenty of fruit, such as sweet ripe apples and green foods (easily supplied in the form of spinach leaves) and they are also fond of the fleshy stalks of the seed-kale variety of beet.

Training

Parrots are undoubtedly the most intelligent of birds but their ability to talk depends on their talent for mimicry rather than their intelligence. They can imitate other sounds as well as the human voice so, if a Parrot is being taught to talk, it should be kept out of earshot of other sounds, e.g. creaking doors, street vendors, radio music. It is the household pet, kept indoors away from other birds, which learns most easily. Males of all species tend to be the most vocal but individual hens of African Greys and Amazons have proved to be exceptional talkers.

Great patience is required on the part of the teacher. A definite time for teaching should be set aside, preferably in the evening, and the lessons should be repeated on the following morning. Enunciate each word clearly and distinctly. In this way, words, and even complete sentences, may be mastered. A bird will learn to associate certain words with certain actions, such as feeding, and will thus give the impression that it is capable of reasoning.

At first your bird will be overheard repeating, as if to itself, the shape rather than the exact words of its lesson. From this point, it will not be long until it can articulate clearly.

Although your bird may be reluctant at first, by coaxing and rewarding it with titbits, your bird will soon be encouraged to talk in front of strangers.

Breeding

Parrot-breeding is a rather specialised occupation, probably best left to the experts. Although Cockatiels have been bred successfully in confined breeding cages, an aviary is really essential if for no other reason than the size of the birds. The same problems tend to occur with Mynah Birds. Parrots are difficult to sex and they are generally kept singly in order to encourage their talking ability. Additionally, in the wild, Parrots tend to mate for life and, if separated from their mates, may be reluctant to take new partners.

In the wild, Parrots nest in holes—in trees, burrows and among roots and rocks. They seldom use any nesting material, apart from the debris occurring naturally in such places. They are gregarious birds and only separate for breeding purposes.

Pairing

African Greys are slow to mature and the hens seldom lay before the age of 4 years. (The majority of imports are hens.) However, once a true pair is obtained and settles down, they will breed fairly readily and young have been reared in cages, aviaries and at liberty.

Cockatiels will also breed readily. Although they mature before the age of 1 year, breeding is best left until the second year. The pair should be put together at least 4 months before the breeding season commences.

Although there have been reports of successful breeding of Amazons and Senegals, these are few and far between. The Senegal was, and still is, fairly inexpensive to import and it was not until the mid-1970s that serious breeding was attempted.

Nesting and incubation

Parrots do not as a rule furnish their chosen nest-sites with nesting material. Their eggs are pure white and round in shape and the clutch ranges from one to five, occasionally as many as eight. The incubation period is approximately 3 weeks and, generally, it is the hen which incubates the eggs while the cock keeps her supplied with food. When hatched, the young parrots are blind and naked but they quickly develop a covering of down.

Both birds are generally excellent parents, feeding (by regurgitation) and caring for the young between them. While feeding the young, the adults should be offered soaked and germinated seed, bread moistened with milk, chopped hard-boiled egg, boiled potato and carrot and soaked millet spray.

It is important to give adequate privacy with only the minimum amount of disturbance necessary to keep the quarters clean.

Figure 32 Parrots will nest in a variety of places

Care of young birds

The chicks are slow to mature and generally remain in the nest for between 4 and 12 weeks. When they do emerge, they are fully feathered and can fly strongly. Nevertheless, the parents usually continue to feed them until they are fully independent. Watch the parents closely for any sign of bullying, in which case the youngsters should be removed.

The Fancy

In the UK, there is in existence a thriving organisation called the Parrot Society which was the first such organisation created to cater for the needs of breeders of Parrot-like birds, since when other similar societies have been formed in various parts of the world. However, the Parrot Society is looked upon as the parent body. It was founded in November 1966 and, from an initial membership of some 250, has grown steadily to its present international membership of 3300. It is a recognised charity, membership of which is open to all persons or organizations interested in its objects. It has as its aims the study and conservation of all Parrots and Parrot-like birds other than domestic Budgerigars. Also, and this may be of interest to new fanciers, every member is entitled to free non-trade advertising in its magazine for wants, sales and exchanges of Parrots (scarce varieties sometimes being offered). It has a medal award scheme not solely confined to first breedings but also for meritorious breeding achievements as determined by the council, and for outstanding contributions to the magazine.

The Parrot Society is always eager to help a beginner, enjoys good contacts with overseas societies and, where possible, holds area meetings for members which can take the form of film shows, lectures, outings or simply get-togethers where fellow hobbyists can discuss their problems and matters of general interest.

5
Mynah Birds

Origins

There are a number of different species of Mynahs, most of which originate from India, South-East Asia, Indonesia and the Phillipines. They belong to the same family as the Starlings and show many similarities in appearance and habits. In their wild state, they nest in holes and crevices in typical starling fashion. All are quite hardy and can be kept out of doors without artificial heat as long as the temperature does not fall below 4°C (40°F). In the wild they live for about 8 years but in captivity they may well live for longer. One captive Mynah is known to have lived for 25 years.

Choosing and buying your Mynah

The majority of Mynahs are imported and are fairly expensive to buy, particularly those which are accomplished talkers. In many cases, they have been hand-fed and are quite tame. Ideally, you should choose a bird between 4 and 6 months.

The Hill Mynahs (*Gracula religiosa*) are by far the most prodigious talkers and hence are very popular. There are several subspecies, ranging in size from the Lesser India Hill Mynah (about the size of a Mistle Thrush) to the Greater India Hill Mynah (roughly the size of a Jackdaw). All adult Hill Mynahs have glossy black plumage with a band of white on the wings. The legs and feet are yellow and the beak is bright orange, becoming paler towards the tip. There are two flaps (wattles) of bare yellow skin extending from just below the eyes to

behind the head. In young birds, the plumage is duller, the beak is paler and the wattles are ivory in colour.

Other Mynah species of interest include the Common Mynah (*Acridotheres tristis*) and the Pagoda and Malabar Mynahs (*Sturnus pagodarum* and *malabaricus*). In the USA, there are restrictions on the import of these three species.

The Common Mynah is rather bigger than the Common Starling. It is dark grey with black and white wings and tail, a yellow beak and rather long yellow legs. Hand-reared specimens make attractive pets and can be taught to say a few words. An instance is recorded of a Common Mynah which escaped from its aviary and spent the whole of an English winter at liberty in the neighbourhood—which speaks well for its hardiness.

The Pagoda Mynah is one of the most prettily-coloured Mynahs.

Above: *Figure 34 The Pagoda Mynah is attractively coloured, blue-grey above and pinkish chestnut below*

Opposite: *Figure 33 The handsome Hill Mynah from India is a prodigious talker*

Smaller than the Common Starling, it is blue-grey above and pinkish chestnut below with a black tail tipped with white. It has a crest of long, backwardly-curling black feathers which rest along the nape of the neck and can be raised and lowered. This little Mynah makes a pretty inmate of an aviary and is a safe companion for other birds of similar size. It has been bred successfully on several occasions. The Malabar Mynah is very similar but lacks a crest. It is pearl-grey above and chestnut below and its head is almost cream.

Accommodation

Cages should be as large as possible because Mynah Birds are very active. The area should be at least 150×60 cm (60×24 in) and the height at least 90 cm (36 in). The cage should be made of metal with a good quality plated finish as otherwise the frequent cleaning necessary will cause it to rust.

Mynah Birds produce copious loose droppings and, ideally, there should be a deep slide-out tray at the bottom, covered by a grill. The tray should be lined with newspaper, sawdust or cat litter to absorb the droppings and any discarded pieces of fruit. (Cat litter or sawdust should only be used if the grill is sufficiently far from the floor to prevent the Mynah Bird from reaching down and accidentally ingesting them.) The grill prevents the Mynah Bird from soiling its feet. The cage should be kept in a draught-free position out of direct sunlight.

Mynah Birds are hardy and can be kept out of doors but the temperature of their quarters should not be allowed to fall below 4°C (40°F).

Figure 35 A deep litter tray is essential in a Mynah cage

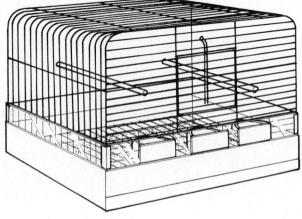

Accessories

There should be at least two perches in the cage so that your bird can get some exercise by jumping from one to the other.

Regular bathing keeps the Mynah Bird's plumage sleek and healthy-looking and a dish holding about 5 cm (2 in) of water should be provided for this purpose. A morning bath is preferable to an evening one so that the bird can dry out completely before it goes to roost. Remove the dish when your bird has finished its bath.

Hygiene

Clean the cage thoroughly once a week, immersing it in water and a mild detergent to loosen any caked-on droppings or bits of food. Rinse it thoroughly and dry it to prevent rusting.

Mynahs clean their beaks on their perches and so these too will need cleaning. Scrape off the worst of the deposits lightly with a knife and then scrub the perches well. Dry them thoroughly before putting them back in the cage.

The tray should be emptied each day and refurbished with newspaper, litter or sawdust. At the same time, you should remove any rotting or mouldy food.

Feeding

Mynah Birds are coarse feeders and in the wild will eat almost any soft plant material but especially fruit.

Since Mynah meal and pellets came onto the market, the problems of diet for the captive bird have been largely overcome. Both meal and pellets contain protein, dehydrated fruit, minerals and vitamins and they form a complete balanced diet on their own. Both meal and pellets can be moistened with water or the pellets can be given in their dry state. As an alternative, dog meal moistened with water and supplemented with vitamins and minerals can be offered.

Extras should be limited to fruits (preferably over-ripe), raw minced meat, grubs, mealworms, insects and the occasional ant's eggs or cocoons and a little hard boiled egg. Berries, such as elder, hawthorn, mountain ash and holly, may also be offered.

Cut down on the extras if your bird begins to eat them in preference to the pellets or meal or its diet will become unbalanced. Avoid giving table scraps because the fats and oils used in cooking may cause digestive problems. Seeds should never be given as Mynahs are unable to digest them.

Mynahs eat constantly so food should always be available and not restricted to one or two 'meals' a day. A constant supply of drinking water is also essential.

Training

A bird between 4 and 6 months is easily tamed but the process gets more difficult as the bird gets older. Mynahs are naturally inquisitive and this can be used to your advantage. Establish your bird's confidence by gentle stroking and rubbing the head feathers before progressing to finger-training (see also p. 17). Hand-feeding will help to establish the relationship. Never tease your bird.

Both male and female Mynahs can be taught to talk with equal facility and, unlike parrots, they are also adept at mimicking tones of voice and speech inflections. Mynahs are such perfect mimics that James Allcock, in his book *A Pet Bird of your Own*, warns that a Mynah placed in the garden within earshot of wild birds may end up singing like a Thrush or chattering like a Magpie.

With regular daily teaching sessions, of about 20 minutes duration, your Mynah should soon accumulate quite an extensive vocabulary. Progress may be slow at first but, once it has acquired a few words, it will begin to learn more rapidly. A word of warning. Do not whistle to your bird if you want it to talk. Mynahs learn to mimic whistling far more easily than speech and may neglect their lessons as a consequence.

Breeding

Early attempts at breeding Mynah Birds were generally unsuccessful because not enough was known about their diet, particularly that of the fledgelings. Even now, Mynahs are rarely bred except in zoos and bird gardens. There are several reasons for this. Most owners keep only one bird, for companionship and its talking ability, and they are reluctant to relegate it to an aviary for breeding. Also sexing Mynahs is not an easy task as the slight difference between the sexes varies with age and condition. There is no shortage of the young Mynahs imported from overseas. These are generally hand-reared and tame and the price is low enough not to offer any incentive to commercial breeders.

Accommodation
Should you have a pair of Mynah Birds which you wish to breed, they should be kept in a secluded aviary at least 3.5×1.2 m (12×4 ft) in area and 1.8 m (6 ft) high. The temperature should not be allowed to fall below 4 °C (40 °F) and heating may be necessary in cooler climates. A nest box 23×23 cm (9×9 in) in area and 38 cm (15 in) high with an entrance hole 7.5 cm (3 in) in diameter should be provided.

Pairing
In the case of the Greater India Hill Mynah, both birds should be at least 3 years old. The smaller species breed when slightly younger. The birds should be installed in the aviary well before the breeding season in order to accustom them to their new quarters. The usual diet should be supplemented with live food.

Nesting and incubation
Nest material in the form of twigs and straw should be given. If mating is successful, the female will lay up to 3 fertile eggs on successive days and these will hatch in about a fortnight. (Should your solitary Mynah lay an egg, do not remove it until she has stopped incubating it as this will only make her lay more.)

Care of young birds
The chicks will begin to show their feathers after about a week and usually leave the nest at 4 weeks of age. By 6 weeks of age they will begin to feed themselves but, unless you intend to hand-feed them, they should be left with their parents. The chicks have voracious appetites and the food provided for them should be particularly rich in protein.

Exhibiting your bird

Mynahs that are in good condition and sleek in feathers can be shown either at a specialist club show or more often in a show organised by a caged bird society. You should make sure that the correct class has been entered, i.e. one for large soft bills in the foreign bird section. The Mynah Bird, unlike most other foreign birds, need not be exhibited in a specific show cage. There is also the advantage, certainly for Mynah owners in the UK, that, although their Mynahs may not be a beauty by show standard, they can still excel themselves by their mimicking ability for, at the National Exhibition of Cage and Aviary Birds, there is a special class for talking Mynahs and the best talking bird.

Preparing your bird for showing

If you are planning to show your Mynah in a standard class, no specific preparation should be necessary provided that its plumage is in first-class condition. If it is not, you can spray the bird at regular intervals for about a fortnight before the date of the show. Do take care that the cage is protected from draughts in transit by putting a cloth over it if necessary.

6
Birds and the law

Before buying any pet, make sure that there are no restrictions on keeping animals in your home. In leasehold and rented properties, there may be a clause in the tenancy agreement precluding the keeping of pets without the written consent of the owner. This may prove to be just a formality but some landlords and councils will not allow pets at all—even small cage birds. Of course, if you are planning to install an aviary in your garden it might be as well to consult your neighbours first!

In the UK, a licence is not necessary to keep a pet bird but if you purchase your bird from a pet-shop, the shop itself must be licensed by the local district council under the Pet Animals Act of 1951. A breeder who sells you a bird, however, is exempt from any such regulation.

Although you may buy birds from pet-shops and breeders quite freely in the UK, it is not so simple to import one from abroad. Until fairly recently, the Ministry of Agriculture, Fisheries and Food allowed individuals to bring back with them from certain overseas countries, birds which had been in their possession for 2 months beforehand, subject to the completion of a simple declaration and to the birds being taken into quarantine in the owner's home for a speci-fied number of days immediately on arrival. This concession has recently been rescinded and, at the moment, anyone attempting to bring a bird into the country without following the correct procedures runs the risk of having the bird confiscated and destroyed. Rules can change, however, within a matter of months and anyone contemplat-ing importing a bird into the UK would be well advised to check the existing position with the Quarantine Division of the MAFF.

The law in the USA is more complicated because it varies from state to state. Advice on the current import regulations can be obtained from the nearest Fish and Wildlife Service District Law Enforcement office. Basically, the restrictions imposed by the US Department of Agriculture apply to certain categories of animals, game birds, poultry and other birds (including hatching birds) and to the entry and inter-state shipment of carriers of animal diseases. Some species are prohibited altogether, while others must be held in a USDA Import Center, or by the owner, for 30—60 days after entry. Only two pet birds can be brought in and these must have been in the owner's possession for 90 days before entry. The Veterinary Services division of the USDA can advise you on any import plans.

Useful addresses

United Kingdom

General

British Bird Breeders Association, 3 Station Road, Lower Stondon, Henlow, Bedfordshire.

Cage and Aviary Birds, Surrey House, 1 Throwley Way, Sutton, Surrey SM1 4QQ.

Ivy Cottage Bird Farm, Turkey Island, Shedfield Common, Nr Southampton, Hampshire (Accessories, seed, aviaries).

Spillers Foods Limited (Caperns Advisory Service), New Malden House, 1 Blagdon Road, New Malden, Surrey.

Budgerigars

Budgerigar Society, 57 Stephyns Chambers, Bank Court, Hemel Hempstead, Hertfordshire.

Pedigree Education Centre (Budgerigar Information Bureau), Pedigree Petfoods Limited, Waltham-on-the-Wolds, Melton Mowbray, Leicestershire LE14 4RS.

Scottish Budgerigar Society, Glenview, Oldmeldrum, Aberdeenshire.

Canaries

British Border Fancy Canary Club, 19 Mona Street, Bootle, Merseyside.

British Roller Canary Association, 9 Mayfair Drive, Royton, Oldham, Lancashire.

British Roller Canary Club, 41 John Aird Court, Howler Place, Paddington, London W2.

Canary Colour Breeders Association, 21 Fairlawn Road, Montpelier, Bristol.

Crested Canary Club, 79 Haslemere Road, Bexleyheath, Kent.

Fife Fancy Canary Specialist Club, 10 Roomin Gardens, Kirkcaldy, Fife, Scotland.

Gloucester Fancy Canary Club, 8 Shurdington Road, Cheltenham, Gloucestershire.

Lizard Canary Association, 18 Lavender Lane, Stourbridge, West Midlands.

National Bengalese Fanciers Association, 18 Nursely Lane, Brechin, Angus, Scotland.

National British Bird and Mule Club, Milnsbridge, Bicton, Nr Shrewsbury.

National Roller Canary Society, 9 Francis Road, Wollaston, Stourbridge, West Midlands.

Norwich Plainhead Canary Club, 11 Robina Wood, Sutton, St Helens, Merseyside.

Scotch Fancy Canary Specialist Club, 14 Schaw Court, Sauchie, Alloa, Scotland.

Yorkshire Canary Club, 3 Como Grove, Girlington, Bradford.

Zebra Finches
Zebra Finch Society, 103 Horncastle Road, Lee, London SE12.

Parrots
Parrot Society, 17 DeParys Avenue, Bedford, Bedfordshire.

United States of America

General
American Association of Zoological Parks and Aquariums, Oglebay Park, Wheeling, WV 26003.

American Federation of Aviculture, PO Box 327, El Cayon, CA 92022.

Greater Northern American Aviculturist and Colourbred Judges Association, 609 Grove Avenue, Edison, NJ 08817.

Pet Producers of America Inc., RT 2 Concordia, KS 66901.

United States Department of Agriculture, Federal Building, Hyattsville, MD 20782.

Budgerigars
American Budgerigar Society, 2 Farnum Road, Warwick, RI 02888.

Canaries
American Border Fancy Canary Club, 21 Gladstone Drive, East Brunswick, NJ 08816.
American Norwich Society, 832 South Franklin Street, Wilkes-Barre, PA 18702.
American Singers Club, 410−31 Barrington Road, Wauconda, IL 60084.
Central States Roller Canary Breeders Association, 505 West McKinley, Havard, IL 60033.
International Border Fancy Canary Club, 1888 Mannering Road, Cleveland, OH 44112.
US Association of Roller Canary Culturists, 3728 Bronx Boulevard, Bronx, NY 10467.
Yorkshire Canary Club of America, 64−50 Admiral Avenue, Middle Village, NY 11379.

Zebra Finches
Toledo Bird Association, Zebra Finch Club of America, 2410 Ida Drive, Toledo, OH 42613.
Zebra Finch Society of America, 8204 Woodland Avenue, Annandale, VA 22003.

Parrots
American Cockatiel Society, 9812 Bois de'Arc Court, Fort Worth, TX 76126.

References

Books

Allcock, J. (1981) *A pet bird of your own* Sheldon Press, London.

Bates, H. and Busenbark, R. (1976) *Parrots and related birds* T.F.H. Publications, Reigate, Surrey.

Low, R. (1976) *Mynah Birds* Bartholomew and Son Ltd, Edinburgh.

Low, R. (1980) *Parrots: their care and breeding* Blandford Press, Poole, Dorset.

Meaden, F. (1979) *A Manual of European bird keeping* Blandford Press, Poole, Dorset.

Paradise, P. R. (1979) *Canaries* T.F.H. Publications, Reigate, Surrey.

Rabtke, G. (1979) *Budgerigars* T.F.H. Publications, Reigate, Surrey.

Rodgers, C. (1977) *Zebra Finches* Bartholomew and Son Ltd, Edinburgh.

Rutgers, A. (1982) *Budgerigars in colour. Their care and breeding* Edited by C. Rogers. Blandford Press, Poole, Dorset.

Rutgers, A. and Norris, K. A. (eds) (1970-77) *Encyclopaedia of aviculture* Vols 1 to 3.

Scoble, J. (1982) *The complete book of Budgerigars* Blandford Press, Poole, Dorset.

Roberts, M. F. (1979) *Society Finches* T.F.H. Publications, Reigate, Surrey.

Stroud, R. (1966) *Diseases of birds* T.F.H. Publications, Reigate, Surrey.

Trollope, J. (1983) *The care and breeding of seed-eating birds* Blandford Press, Poole, Dorset.

Vriends, T. (1980) *Cage and aviary birds* Ward Lock, London.

Walker, G. (1976) *Coloured Canaries* Blandford Press, Poole, Dorset.

Periodicals

American Cage Bird Magazine (c/o 3449 North Western Avenue, Chicago, Illinois.)

Bird World (c/o 1152 Hartsooh Street, North Hollywood, California 9601.)

Cage and Aviary Birds Surrey House, 1 Throwley Way, Sutton, Surrey SM1 4QQ.)

Index